Just Dying To Live

Renewal Through a Review of Romans

JIM HYLTON

MASTER'S PRESS, INC.

All biblical quotations are taken from the King James Version unless otherwise noted.

Acknowledgment is given for:

Permission to quote from the *Amplified Bible* published by Zondervan Publishing House, Grand Rapids, Michigan, copyright 1965.

Excerpt from *If I Die* by B. McCall Barbour. Copyright by B. McCall Barbour, Edinburgh, Scotland. Used by permission.

Quotation from *The Secret of Soul Winning*, by Dr. Stephen F. Olford, published by Moody Press, Chicago, Illinois. Copyright 1963. Used by permission.

Quotation from *Studies in the Bible and Science*, by Henry Morris, published by Presbyterian and Reformed Publishing Company, Nutley, New Jersey. Copyright 1966. Used by permission.

Quotation from *God's Grace* by Donald Grey Barnhouse. Published by William B. Eerdmans Publishing Co., Grand Rapids, Michigan. Copyright 1959. Used by permission.

JUST DYING TO LIVE
ISBN # 0-89251-008-0

Published by Master's Press, Inc.
20 Mills Street, Kalamazoo, MI

Published in the United States of America

DEDICATION

To Jane, with whom I've shared the companion-ship of life twenty-one years and the in-depth companionship of the Christ-life for the last ten years.

To Lyn, Debby, Randy, and Lea Ann, who have been understanding and encouraging team members in my travelling to tell others.

To Dad and Mother, who first told me who Christ is and then led me to know Him.

To the Start Living Now Crusade family, who have faithfully prayed for the completion of this book and are part of my ministry every-where.

PREFACE

The power of the Word of God to transform human lives is the miracle of the ages. Nowhere has that marvelous power been more clearly demonstrated than in the amazing conversions and spiritual renewals which have been brought about by the study of the Epistle of Paul to the Romans.

Augustine, in the fourth century, was deeply convicted by the simple words of a child at play beyond the walls of his garden, "Take up and read! Take up and read!" Receiving this as a divine sign for his troubled soul, he took up the Bible and it fell open to the last verses of Romans 13—"Let us walk honestly, as in the day; not in rioting and drunkenness, not in chambering and wantonness, not in strife and envying. But put ye on the Lord Jesus Christ, and make not provision for the flesh, to fulfil the lusts thereof." The words convicted a profligate sinner, and Augustine turned from a life of debauchery and shame to become a new creature in Christ. He blessed the world with some of the greatest theological writings in the whole history of Christendom.

In a time of tremendous spiritual renewal in many of our churches today, Evangelist Jim Hylton has been used of God to teach and preach the thrilling message of *Romans* and all of God's

Holy Book to thousands of people in America and overseas. Now he has put the heart of his original study of the Roman Epistle into a book; and, like any effective book, it vibrates with the author's own experience. It has been my privilege to see the transforming power of God's Spirit in the life and ministry of Jim Hylton. It revolutionized his prayer life and permeated his family, his church, and the whole community. It touched my life, many hundreds of miles away. I believe that his sensitivity to the impression of the Holy Spirit and his faithful persistence in prayer had a part in saving my life, and the life of eighty other people. In a series of strange events, too involved to chronicle, I stopped a commercial flight from taking off in Dallas, Texas. Minutes later the mechanics confirmed a control malfunction which would have meant almost certain disaster. After I was safely home on another flight, the phone rang, and it was Jim Hylton, saying, "Dr. Ward, are you all right?" Because of a strong impression that I was in great need or great danger, Jim had been in his study praying during those morning hours when our lives were hanging in the balance. Did God use the prayer obedience of his servant to work a miracle of deliverance? I believe so; and I believe that when we are not sensitive to God's impression and when we are not faithful in prayer, we hinder the mighty power of God from working in our lives. Remember the people at Nazareth—Jesus *could not* do any mighty work there because of their unbelief!

Out of such a life of transforming experience with the Spirit of God this book has come. In *Just Dying to Live*, Jim Hylton has drawn from the deep well of the Roman letter and shares divinely given insights in the most practical and helpful way. It is written so that any sincere individual can be strengthened and enriched by these blessings from the Word of God. Or, a pastor might use it as a guide and take his people through an intensive study of the kind of Christian life which can open up before any believer who completely yields himself to the power of the transforming and renewing Word of God. I recommend this book, with deep gratitude, to every one who is seriously searching for a more meaningful life in the Lord. At many places it will confirm and illuminate your own experience; at others it will surprise and challenge you to a new and more vital life as a Christian. May the transforming power of God renew your life and plant a new song upon your lips as you study through these pages!

Wayne Ward
Southern Baptist Seminary
Louisville, Kentucky
May, 1976

CONTENTS

FOREWORD

"Just Dying to Live" has been the personal experience of Jim Hylton for the past ten years. I witnessed the agony as the process of death to self set in at a pastor's retreat in Van Buren, Missouri. Jim bowed his face to the floor and wept as he acknowledged the dominating power of self and the flesh in his life. The transformation did not take place instantly, it never does, but the cyclical process was started. It took several weeks to sort out the elements of frustration, hostility, pride, jealousy, hypocrisy etc. This was the breaking, dying to self period, then came the unconditional surrender to the Lordship of Jesus Christ.

This book is not a critical commentary on a section of the Epistle to the Romans. It is a practical guide to the victorious life in Christ based upon Romans, chapter 5 through 8. It is an accurate interpretation of what the Holy Spirit communicated through the apostle Paul to the saints of Rome and to us. For the past decade Jim Hylton has preached and lived the realities set forth in this book.

James H. Smith, Executive Secretary
Illinois Baptist State Association
Springfield, Illinois

INTRODUCTION

Accept this as your invitation to take a journey
with me into an experience of normal Christian
living. The itinerary calls for a look at the "heart-
land" of the Bible, the book of Romans. While all
scriptural roads, when followed, lead to renewal,
the book of Romans uniquely gives us a guide to
the destination. A journey into renewal that by-
passes Romans results in a discovery sooner or
later that Romans and Renewal are like Siamese
twins; one can't be born without the other. From
continent to continent, from culture to culture,
across centuries, you see the book of Romans leading people to renewal, and renewal leading people
to the book of Romans.

From the classroom of mental acquaintance to
the laboratory of living experience, I have viewed
its majestic truths. Ten years ago I began
preaching through the book. The result was spiritual revolution in my own life and revival in the
church where I served as pastor. Seven years ago I
began a traveling ministry that has resulted in my
teaching this book over 150 times. Each trip into
this treasure house of riches has called for me to
carry away some new-found understanding of
value. I never journey in its pages without dislodg-
ing some new nugget of glowing importance.

Even though I have given "re-runs of the re-runs," these messages have never grown stale in my heart.

The testimonies of others who have made these passages of Romans to be patterns for their lives give similar accounts. Godet, the Swiss commentator, makes this observation: "In studying it we find ourselves, at every word, face to face with the unfathomable . . . it is probable that every great spiritual renovation in the church will always be linked, both in cause and in effect, to a deeper knowledge of this book." Martin Luther writes, "The epistle to the Romans is the true masterpiece of the New Testament and the very purest gospel . . . man should not only learn it by heart, word for word, but also . . . daily deal with it as the daily bread of men's souls. It can never be too much or too well read or studied, and the more it is handled the more precious it becomes, and the better it tastes." Another concluding example is John Bunyan, author of the classic *Pilgrim's Progress*, whose life was revolutionized by studying the book of Romans. With his body locked in a prison, the simple Bedford tinker let his spirit and mind tour those passages of Scripture. The result was a transformation of his life, and, ultimately, the book *Pilgrim's Progress* that has served as a guide to Christians across the centuries.

You will locate Romans at a conspicuous place in the New Testament. The four Gospels and the book of Acts show Christ coming to us and indwelling us. In all five accounts He is seen in a human body. The last of the five books, Acts, portrays a combination of bodies making up His collective body—the Church. Then comes Romans. It's as though the greatest celebrity of all times has been presented, and suddenly a guide to "How to Know Him" has been thrust into your hands. As a distillation of concentrated truth, Romans shows us how to enter into Christ's life and benefit fully from all His accomplishments.

Having traveled and talked with many fellow pilgrims in journeys into Romans, I am truly "a part of all I have met." I acknowledge my indebtedness to many whom I have heard speak and whom I have read. The three men contributing most to me have been Donald Grey Barnhouse, Watchman Nee, and Stuart Briscoe.

A special thank-you is included to Mrs. Susie Whitsell for capably and conscientiously typing the manuscript.

THE PRIVILEGE OF EVERY CHRISTIAN

Romans 5:1–8

One of the richest oil fields in West Texas was once the scene of dire poverty. The oil field is known as the Yates Pool.

A sheep rancher named Yates and his family eeked out an existence on the land. Caught in the midst of the great depression of the 1930's, they were in danger of losing the entire ranch. Only government relief kept them in operation. Day by day Mr. Yates grazed the sheep on hills of West Texas with worry as his companion. His worry over how he would pay his bills prohibited any enjoyment of life or of the ranch and the land about him.

One day a survey crew from an oil company came by and told Mr. Yates they thought there might be oil on the ranch. They asked for drilling rights, and he signed the contract. When the drilling began, they struck a gusher at 1,115 feet. The well produced 80,000 barrels a day. Wells that followed could produce twice that capacity. Even thirty years later government surveys showed wells with a capacity for 125,000 barrels a day.

Mr. Yates owned it all! When he purchased the

land the oil came with it. During all his years of poverty, he was rich and didn't know it. All the days of toil and worry were spent in the presence of riches. Years elapsed before Mr. Yates possessed what he owned and enjoyed his privileges of ownership. A multimillionaire had lived on government relief checks.

The privilege of every Christian is to go from the rags of poverty to the riches of Christ's abundance. The wells of wealth untold belong to every Christian. We will see how to locate and enjoy our riches in Christ. Our first stop will be at the "sheep ranch" of spiritual poverty without Christ. Then we will see how to claim all of our rights in Christ!

Since our first stop is well into the book of Romans, we must locate ourselves in reference to what we have already passed by. The first word in Romans 5 reveals a sign pointing backward, then forward. THEREFORE is one of the most important words in scripture. Discovering what every "therefore" is THERE FOR is necessary in good Bible study. The Bible deals with principles, then application. The "therefores" are the transitional words that take us from the classroom of knowing about it to the laboratory of discovering how it works.

A quick glance back into chapters 1 and 2 reveals man's sin problem. God and man are separated. "*God gave them up*" is written like an epitaph over scenes of sin. Spiritual conditions grow worse as chapter 3 begins. Concentrate on verses 9-18:

What then? Are we better than they? No, in no wise: for we before proved both Jews and Gentiles, that they are all under sin; As it is written, There is none righteous, no not one: There is none that understandeth, there is none that seeketh after God. They are all gone out of the way, they are together become un-profitable; there is none that doeth good, no, not one. Their throat is an open sepulchre; with their tongues they have used deceit; the poison of asps is under their lips; Whose mouth is full of cursing and bitterness: Their feet are swift to shed blood: Destruction and misery are in their ways: And the way of peace have they not known: There is no fear of God before their eyes. Comfortless and without excuse we see that their ways are our ways: *"For all have sinned and come short of the glory of God"* (Romans 3:23).

Suddenly a quick turn in truth's tour brings us to the brow of a hill where man's plight was remedied by Jesus Christ.

> "Jesus paid it all
> All to Him I owe
> Sin had left a crimson stain
> He washed it white as snow."

"Being justified freely by his grace through the re-demption that is in Christ Jesus" (Romans 3:24). *"Therefore we conclude that a man is justified by faith apart from the deeds of the law"* (Romans 3:28). Having looked back ever so briefly, we can turn our attention with even greater appreciation to the privileges we have as Christians.

THE PRIVILEGE OBTAINED

"Therefore being justified by faith we have peace with God through our Lord Jesus Christ" (Romans 5:1). It is faith in Jesus Christ plus nothing, minus nothing, that brings us to enjoy PEACE WITH GOD. God's person of salvation is a person of peace, Jesus Christ, the Prince of Peace. It is not a plan that makes us a Christian, but a person. It is not a system that makes us a Christian, but a Savior Himself. Put a plus sign after Christ and you have a system or a plan of works such as baptism, church membership, or man's morality. Put up a minus sign after Christ and you try to make Christ less than He is. He is either all He said or He is nothing He said. As Dr. William R. Bright has said, "He is either Lord of Heaven and Earth, or He is a liar, or a lunatic."

Being a Christian involves a unique relationship with Jesus Christ, God's person of salvation. You can generally determine immediately if you have encountered Christianity or mere religion by the direction in which it moves. Religion always moves from man toward God. Christianity moves from God toward man in Jesus Christ. If man is initiating it, you can mark it as religion only. If God has initiated it in Christ, then you can regard it as Christianity.

Dr. J. Edwin Orr's explanation of Christianity will illustrate our relationship with Christ. At the University of Chicago, a young lady brought up a question: "I don't understand this. If a man believes in Communism, he is a Communist; if he believes in Socialism, he is a Socialist. Well, I believe in Christianity—am I not a Christian?"

"Not necessarily so," Dr. Orr replied. Facetiously, he relates, he asked the young ladies in the company present how many of them believed in marriage, and they all happily raised their hands—except one determined spinster.

"That's very interesting," he said. "You all say that you believe in marriage as an institution or a philosophy. This young lady says if one believes in Communism, he is a Communist; if one believes in Christianity, he is a Christian. Now you all tell me you believe in marriage. Allow me to pronounce you married."

That statement was greeted with hoots of derision.

"What's wrong with that?" he asked.

"Mr. Orr," protested one girl, "you know that marriage is not a philosophy; marriage is a personal relationship!"

"Exactly," he returned. "And Christianity is

not a mere philosophy. Being a Christian is a personal relationship with Jesus Christ, a living person."

In Jesus Christ, God has purchased our perfect salvation. We are then justified by faith. Faith appropriates what God has already allocated for us. It is not even faith in faith that saves us, but faith in Jesus Christ. The most workable definition of faith I know is the one given by Vance Havner. Making faith into an acrostic, he defined it as meaning:

F orsaking
A ll
I
T rust
H im

Saving faith involves forsaking sin, self, and systems to trust Christ to be IN us all that He has already been FOR us. That kind of faith has no parallel to our exercise of faith in other realms. Simply because we exercise a natural faith in cars to take us to our destination, or in the principle of areodynamics to keep our plane aloft for a safe arrival, we can't come to Christ with that same kind of faith and be a Christian. Being a Christian involves forsaking all else and trusting Christ. Many evangelists have erroneously admonished people to trust Christ casually just as they have trusted their cars to carry them or the church pews to hold them. Many respond but do not become Christians. They are numbered among the decisions but are never noticed among the disciples. Trusting Christ can never be casual; it always involves crisis, the crisis of forsaking all to trust Him.

If any of the following study is to make spiritual sense, it is essential to establish now that you are a Christian. Becoming a Christian is profoundly simple and simply profound. A confessed sinner receives a confirmed Savior and becomes a credentialed Christian. Our contribution is to furnish a sinner. God's contribution is to furnish a Savior, who then furnishes everything. Sinners make wonderful Christians because Christ gives us the *"power to become"* (John 1:12).

THE PRIVILEGE CONTAINED
"By whom also we have access by faith into this grace wherein we stand and rejoice in hope of the glory of God" (Romans 5:2).

Through Continuation of Faith

Every Christian is a container of Christ's own life. *"Christ in you is the hope of glory"* (Colossians 1:27). *"We have this treasure in earthen vessels that the excellency of the power may be of God and not us"* (2 Corinthians 4:7). Now as containers of Christ, we have received His grace and are privileged to gain access to all God's provisions on our behalf. Just as by faith we begin the Christian journey, so by faith we continue the Christian life. YOU BEGAN BY FAITH; NOW PROCEED BY FAITH are the simple instructions for the further journey. The Bible uses three important words to mark the beginning, continuation, and culmination of the Christian life: they are justification, sanctification, and glorification.

In JUSTIFICATION we have been saved from the PENALTY of sin.

In SANCTIFICATION we are being saved from the POWER of sin.

In GLORIFICATION we shall be saved from the PRESENCE of sin.

In justification, we do the letting and Jesus Christ does the saving. Let's skip sanctification for a moment. In glorification, we let Christ take us from our bodies, or in our bodies to heaven and His second coming. No amount of arm waving or jumping will aid Him at all. So no church has even thought of a second coming calisthenics course. You can't jump high enough to be glorified, even with the aid of a trampoline. We will do the letting and He will do the lifting. Since in justification we do the letting and Christ does the saving, and in glorification we do the letting and Christ does the lifting, so in sanctification we do the letting and Christ does the living. "*The just shall live by faith*" (Romans 1:27).

Through a Condition of Grace

So watch your faith, not your step, as we proceed in the grace of God. Limitless and exhaustless are the privileges that are ours through God's grace. The most unexplored frontier awaiting discovery today is the mighty expanse of grace. It stretches before us like a mighty ocean. We have only touched the shoreline.

A few years ago I flew from San Francisco to Sydney, Australia. The entire 18-hour journey was over the expansive Pacific Ocean. A few months after returning to the States I was ministering in San Juan Capistrano, California. Some friends there suggested a break one day for a fishing trip. The guide took us over to a spot just off the coast and we anchored in view of the Nixons' San Clemente home. For hours we concentrated on that spot where fish were reported to be. Watching while someone ever so infrequently pulled up a tiny fish, I thought of the vast expanse of that ocean and the endless possibilities for adventure we were missing by being anchored in that one spot. It reminded me that many Christians have settled down to one spot in their journey and have missed so much.

Through a Concentration on Rejoicing

After moving into grace, we are then to move on, rejoicing in hope of the glory. Once we discover the provisions of God and partake of them by faith, we have no problem reaching the rejoicing realm. The life of rejoicing is the main theme of the Book of Philippians. Look at Philippians 4:4-7:

> *Rejoice in the Lord alway: and* [in case you slept through that, he repeats with emphatic repetition] *again I say, Rejoice. Let your moderation be known unto all men. The Lord is at hand. Be careful for nothing; but in every thing by prayer and supplication with thanksgiving let your requests be made known unto God. And the peace of God, which passeth all understanding, shall keep your hearts and minds through Christ Jesus.*

That scripture experienced would virtually empty counselors' offices around the world. Here is the when, why, how, and what of rejoicing:

When to rejoice .... Always,

Why rejoice .... The Lord is at hand (actually in you).

How to rejoice .... In prayer with thanksgiving, making requests known to God.

What rejoicing brings .. *"The peace of God, which passeth all understanding, shall keep your hearts and minds through Christ Jesus."* (Phil. 4:7).

Through a Confirmation of Glory

"The hope of Glory" is the anticipation of the Lord Himself declaring His person and presence. Glory is the SHEKINAH or fiery presence of God seen as a fire by night and a cloud of smoky splendor by day throughout the Bible. When the glory comes, God has come. We can live aware of His indwelling glory within us. We can live anticipating His declared glory about us. We can live awaiting His coming glory in the air as He comes for us. When revival comes, glory comes. Christians are the first to be aware. Then the lost suddenly become conscious of it.

Duncan Campbell has told in conferences how revival came to the Hebrides Islands near Scotland's coast in 1949. He tells of the glory of God engulfing a whole island one night. He had left a Bible conference on an adjoining island where he was the featured speaker, explaining simply that he had to obey the urging of the Lord to go to the Island of Berneray. Upon arriving, he learned that the services were already set for 9 o'clock that night and he had been announced as the speaker. A layman had prayed and asked God to bring revival. Being impressed that Duncan Campbell should come to minister the Word, he simply said that if the Lord sent Brother Campbell, he would announce the services. Without human communication, he had acted in faith. The service was not unusual, Duncan Campbell recalled, though a sense of freedom prevailed. After the service a prayer meeting was called, and Duncan Campbell was admonished by the layman not to be discouraged. As they started homeward, suddenly the layman, postmaster of the village, slipped to Campbell's side and said, "Stand still Brother Campbell, stand still. The Lord has come, the Lord has come!" Duncan Campbell said as he stopped he became conscious of waves of the presence of God flowing about him. People were being awakened from a sound sleep to get sins confessed and be converted to Christ. He said, "I question there was one single house on the island that was not visited that night." Yes, we are to be aware of indwelling glory within us, anticipating His declared glory about us. REJOICE, REJOICE, REJOICE!!!

THE PRIVILEGE MAINTAINED

Fasten your seat belt before reading the next verses:

And not only so, but we glory in tribulations also: knowing that tribulation worketh patience; and patience, experience; and experience, hope; and hope maketh not ashamed (Romans 5:3-5a).

The transition is so abrupt, you can hardly get your eyes off the scene of glory to face tribulation. In verses one and two you climb the majestic peaks with Paul to stand exultingly ultimately in glory. Then one step later you are back at the kitchen sink with your hands in the dishwater of tribulation.

Tribulation is a word registered among the heavyweights. In the original language it is the word THILIPSIS. It means intensive pressure producing brokenness. Ours has been accurately described as a pressure cooker age. We live daily in the THILIPSIS of the demands made upon us. A process used in Bible times gave birth to the word THILIPSIS or tribulation. The olive and wine presses in the Old Testament produced a pressure that resulted in the flow of a desired quality—the oil from the olive, juice from the grape. In the process both the olive and the grape were crushed or broken. The products of this pressure became symbols of the person and presence of the Lord. In Psalm 104:15 these symbols are capsulated in one verse: *"And wine maketh glad the heart of man, and oil to make his face to shine. . . ."* In Psalm 23 is a reference to both in the overflowing cup and the anointing of the head with oil.

In the Scriptures, oil was used for medicinal purposes but was primarily a cosmetic. People thought of the Lord as the God of a shining face and they desired the same characteristic for themselves, to be like Him. This was achieved by liberally applying olive oil to their faces. Notice the benediction of Moses spoken to Aaron in Numbers 6:24-26: *"The Lord bless thee, and keep thee: The Lord make his face shine upon thee, and be gracious unto thee: The Lord lift up his countenance upon thee, and give thee peace."* God is the God of a shining face. Those who have had deep encounters with Him have always come away with faces shining. Moses on Sinai encountered God and came away with a shining face. Peter, James, and John on the mountain of transfiguration saw Christ's face shine as the sun and they came away with shining faces. Paul marching militantly to Damascus breathing threats and slaughter was met by the Christ of a shining face. He was left blinded for three days. When the scales fell from his eyes, he beheld with appreciation that face reflecting the glory of God.

Paul's experience with the glory of the Lord has direct application to why we are to glory in tribulation. He explains in 2 Corinthians 3:16-18:

Nevertheless when it shall turn to the Lord, the veil shall be taken away. Now the Lord is that Spirit: and where the Spirit of the Lord is, there is liberty. But we all, with open face beholding as in a glass the glory [shining face] of the Lord, are changed into the same image from glory to glory, even as by the Spirit of the Lord.

Just as the olive and the grape are crushed in THILIPSIS and the desired quality flows out, we with an unveiled face in brokenness behold the glory of the Lord and are changed into the same image by the Spirit of the Lord. A desired quality—the Holy Spirit—is in us awaiting release. Not until we are broken can the face be unveiled for the release of the Spirit from within. Then the awareness of the glory of the Lord will be manifest. The Christ of a shining face is still creating a people of shining faces. Those who are beholding glory are being changed into the same image.

In the experience of tribulation, the degree of pressure required is determined by the amount of resistance we offer. The two sides of the same coin are brokenness and yieldedness. If we yield, we are broken voluntarily. If we resist, it may require intensive pressure to break us so we will finally capitulate to Christ's control. We may be broken from without as situations that we can't handle close in about us. Or we may be broken from within as we can no longer bear to endure the desperate emptiness of a life not ruled by Christ.

We are to glory further in tribulation because it is but one stop on the journey back to "hope of the glory." The Christian life involves the cyclical as well as the progression on a straight line. As we have already seen, we move on a continuum from Justification through Sanctification to Glorification. That would best be charted as a straight line with many circles in it. Some circles will be larger than others, thus taking longer to complete. Have you ever said, "I feel that I am going in circles"?

You feel you are going in circles because you are. While moving in the cycle of spiritual growth you may appear to be going backward. You may even think, "If I don't slow down, I'll back right over something."

Let's look at the full cycle. See the circle as the face of a clock. At 12 o'clock we have hope; then from that enjoyable position we are plunged into pressure or tribulation at 3 o'clock. From there we move down to 6 o'clock where we have patience or endurance, and that starts us back on an upward spiral to 9 o'clock where we enjoy experience. The experience leads to more hope and we find ourselves right back where we started at 12 o'clock. Once you learn this cycle you will understand what's going right when tribulation comes and pressure mounts. You can rejoice right through every station on the clock.

When another cycle starts in your life and progress seems to be reversed, remember that God is not in as big a hurry as we are. Dr. A. H. Strong said, "When God wants to make an oak, He takes a hundred years, but when He wants to make a squash, He only takes six months." A "squash" Christian will be squashed in the time of tribulation, but a rejoicing Christian will go on to be the sturdy oak of spiritual stability.

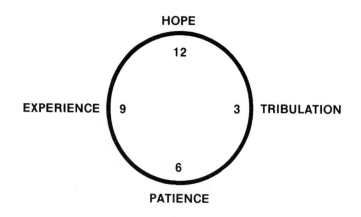

THE PRIVILEGE SUSTAINED

"And hope maketh not ashamed; because the love of God is shed abroad in our hearts by the Holy Ghost . . ." (Romans 5:5). God maintains us in the cycle, and then sustains us through the experiential release of His love in us. God's love is shed abroad in the heart, not in the head. It is not known by merely knowing about it. You cannot measure the love of God by stacking Bible verse upon Bible verse in your mind. John 3:16 can be quoted forward and backward, then split in the middle and quoted in both directions without being a recording of God's love in your heart. Reading and memorizing Elizabeth Barrett Browning's love sonnets to Robert Browning does not allow you to experience her love. Now if she

could enter your heart and share her depths of affection, you would then experience her profound love. This is exactly the role of the Holy Spirit. He enters us to bring God's love within. He is released in us to make God's love experiential.

Most people have difficulty in believing that God really likes them, much less loves them. Yet the greatest need of the human personality is to be loved. God has the original design of love. The Holy Spirit has the distributing rights on His love. We are the showcases of His love. Charles G. Finney described this release of God's love in him as "waves of liquid love pouring over me." We discover God's love as the Holy Spirit sheds it abroad in our hearts. This leads to a disclosure of God's love through our lives.

THE PRIVILEGE ORDAINED

"But God commendeth his love toward us, in that, while we were yet sinners, Christ died for us" (Romans 5:8).

God has ordained unconditional love for us. We are not loved BECAUSE . . . we are not loved IF . . . we are not loved WHEN . . . we are not loved conditionally at all. Even though we were sinners with hearts closed to Him, God came to us with His heart wide open with love.

God said, "I love you" in John 3:16.

God showed He loved you in Romans 5:8.

God showers that love over you in Romans 5:5.

THE POSSESSIONS OF EVERY CHRISTIAN

Romans 5:9–20

The average Christian settles for MUCH LESS than the MUCH MORE of his possessions in Christ. Christ gives us not only the power to get out of sin's bondage, but the privilege of entering into God's abundance. Since hindsight is always 20-20, looking back at the mistakes of others can improve our vision for finding our way to God's total provisions. We can't afford to stop short, as others have done, of possessing our rightful possessions. In Hebrews 3:7-9 we are warned to monitor carefully what the Holy Spirit says to us. The spiritual S.O.S. is given:

> The time is today, vs. 7;
> The truth is to be heard, vs. 8;
> The test is to be passed, vs. 9.

The Time Is Today

God's people had their "today" when they stood at Kadesh Barnea and saw before them the lush land of God's provision. God's time is always "today." Our today is right now.

The Truth Is To Be Heard

When truth came to the Israelites they hardened their hearts instead of hearing with their hearts. The voice of God is *"a still small voice"* (1 King 19:12). We hear God intuitively in our hearts. It requires getting still (having a quiet time) and being small (admitting we are nothing). But instead of getting still and being small enough to hear God speak, we often hear with our heads (the intellect alone) and miss hearing the Lord. God said to the two and one half million newly emancipated people, *"Behold the Lord thy God hath set the land before thee: go up and possess it, as the Lord God of thy fathers hath said unto thee; fear not, neither be discouraged"* (Deuteronomy 1:21). The people said they would prefer for a committee to survey the land and bring a feasibility report. Their reasoning was manward and not Godward. They were MEN ALONE, with MINDS ALONE, GOING ALONE to get a report about what they thought could be done. They should have been MEN ALONG WITH GOD, with MINDS ALONG WITH THE HOLY SPIRIT'S voice GOING ALONG WITH GOD'S REPORT to go up and possess the land. When the committee of twelve returned, ten men said, "We can't," and only two said, "We can." The dreaded spiritual disease identified as the paralysis of analysis had gripped them. Mental analysis without the guidance of

God results in hardness of heart. When we have a hard heart we become hard of hearing spiritually.

The Test Is To Be Passed

Since they were so drowsy in the classroom and heard almost nothing, the children of Israel arrived at the lab session to conduct the test and blew it altogether. The result was forty years of finding out that their way didn't work. In flunking the test they became part of that third of the class that makes the upper two thirds possible.

God calls out, "Don't make the same mistake!"

There remaineth therefore a rest to the people of God. For he that is entered into his rest, he also hath ceased from his own works, as God did from his. Let us labour [be diligent] *therefore to enter into that rest lest any man fall after the same example of unbelief* (Hebrews 4:9-11).

FOLLOW THE FOUR MUCH MORE SIGNS TO ABUNDANCE

1. The MUCH MORE of His Saving Life

Triumphantly the Scripture announces in Romans 5:9, there is MUCH MORE. Carefully the Scripture lays the foundation for the proper appropriation of the MUCH MORE. Notice the three levels of that foundation in verses 9 and 10:

a. Justified by His blood.
b. Saved from wrath through Him.
c. Once we were enemies, now we are reconciled to God by the death of His son.

With the foundation carefully laid, we are ready for the MUCH MORE of His saving life.

For many years if someone had asked me how a person is saved, I would have given a good scriptural account of the saving death of Christ. I would have correctly explained how the Lamb of God, Christ, took my sin and its penalty of death upon Himself so I could take righteousness from Him. He had no sin, yet He took sin for me. I had no righteousness, yet I took it from Him as 2 Corinthians 5:21 reveals: *"For he hath made him, who knew no sin to be sin for us, that we might be made the righteousness of God in Him."* My answer would have been correct, yet woefully incomplete. As the song affirms: "There's more, so much more, than that first sweet day. More so much more, every passing day." We are also saved by HIS LIFE. Like a pearl of great price, the beauty of this prize truth of all truths concerning the Christian life gleams forth. But unlike the pearl of great price, we need not sell all other truths to possess it.

What His Saving Life Saves Us From

In His saving death we are saved from our sins.

In His saving life we are saved from ourselves. "It's fun being saved" has been refuted by people who have been saved but aren't experiencing joy any longer. The testimony of too many is "I was saved two years ago and it was wonderful . . ." or "I was saved twenty years ago and it was so good then . . ." and each time you wait for more but there is no more. You want to ask, "What about now? Isn't it wonderful now?" but you are afraid to. One look immediately reveals that being saved is no longer exciting for them. There is no more to their testimony because they have not found the MUCH MORES of the Scripture. The joy of being saved is being saved by His life. "It's fun to be saved by His life" is the daily testimony of those who are experiencing it. When we are saved daily from ourselves to enjoy His life in us, we are saved from the contemptible qualities of our lives so we can enjoy the satisfying qualities of Christ's life. It must be a daily experience. We are saved by His death once, for He died once; but we are saved by His saving life daily, for He lives daily.

Several years ago I spent a meaningful week in an outstanding church in greater St. Louis, Missouri. It's the oldest evangelical church west of the Mississippi. Wally and Laura Jo Jones had ably graced the church as pastor and pastor's wife for eight rewarding years. Laura Jo was greatly respected as the first lady of the church. Wally had the respect not only of the church, but of pastors and church leaders throughout the nation.

One day during my week with them, Laura Jo asked if she could share a testimony with me so she could clarify scripturally what had "happened to her." Her story was not unlike hundreds of others. She had grown weary of "business as usual," and the meetings and activities she dutifully attended as the pastor's wife had lost their meaning. She was no longer content to live a ho-hum Christian life.

With a characteristic discipline, she had started a quiet time each morning before the family arose. For her reading she selected the Gospel of Mark. Days of keeping tryst with the Lord in the Scriptures brought her to Mark's account of the crucifixion. Being an imaginative person, she projected herself into the account and asked what she would have done on the occasion of the death of Christ. Her conclusion was shocking! She realized that as a professing Christian, even a promoting Christian, when the cross came into view, she would have played it safe and would not have identified with Christ there.

That realization led to days of depression. One morning during her quiet time, she cried out to the Lord, "I don't know what it will be like to go with You to the cross, but I am willing. Take me now! Take all my life now!" The curtain of depression lifted and Christ's life became hers. She said, "I was conscious of Christ in a way I had never been. I spent all day aware of Him, enjoying Him, talking with Him." When Wally returned that evening from the usual activities-filled day, she told him of her most memorable day yet lived. Then she said to him, "I guess for the first time in my life I have met Jesus, for I never knew Him like this before." Then she asked, "If it's true I never met Him until now, it would be true I have never been scripturally baptized, wouldn't it?" He affirmed that she was correct in assuming she had not been baptized properly if Christ was not in her life at the time.

To the surprise of hundreds of worshippers the next Sunday, Laura Jo confessed Christ publicly and that night the pastor baptized his wife before the amazed but pleased church.

In relating this story to me she paused for a moment and said, "But several weeks after being baptized, I realized I did receive Christ as a young lady and had really known Him across the years since. At times He was real to me, but never in a lasting way. I've shared this," she said, "to ask you what happened to me."

I answered her with the question, "How many times since that day six months ago has it seemed that you got saved?" Her eyes lighted with joy when she reflected and said, "Why, every day it's just like I get saved." I said, "The reason it seems like you get saved every day . . . is that you do. The reason it seemed you got saved six months ago . . . is that you did. You were saved by His saving life and daily you are being saved by His saving life." Laura Jo found "IT'S FUN BEING SAVED BY HIS SAVING LIFE."

What His Saving Life Saves Us For

Not only do we experience His saving life, but we also experience joy ringing like bells in the heart. The designs of the Christian life called for joy to be a continuous characteristic. "... *Not only so, but we also joy in God through our Lord Jesus Christ, by whom we have now received the atonement*" (Romans 5:11). Now joy and happiness are quite different. Joy looks to the unchanging person of Jesus Christ. Happiness looks to happenings. When things happen as we want them to happen, happiness remains our companion. But when things don't happen to happen as we want them to happen, we lose the fickle companion called happiness. Joy, however, is our companion even when things are happening that we do not desire. Since Jesus is our companion in times of distress and our joy looks to Him, joy remains faithfully with us.

David lost the joy of his salvation after he sinned. Through confession, God restored his lost joy (Psalm 51). It is the desire of the Lord to restore joy to you if you are not experiencing it. The epistle of John was written so that you may achieve God's objective for you: "... *that your joy may be full*" (1 John 1:4). God's concern for your joy can be seen in Nehemiah 8:10. During a time of revival under Ezra, God said, "*The joy of the Lord is your strength*." Wells of joy are waiting to flow in you because God is wanting their flow for you.

2. The MUCH MORE of His Abounding Grace

What One Man Did To Wrong the Right

Through one man the human personality was corrupted with sin's carnal character. One man marred the masterful work of God. As a knitted garment can all but be destroyed by pulling one loose string, so the garment of God's creation was marred forever by one man's sin. That man, Adam, has little written about him in Scripture, yet we know some things. God created him to take dominion over creation. His brilliant career was brief. In faith he rested in sleep while God created his companion. His uncomplaining acceptance of Eve reveals his wisdom. His unerring accuracy in naming every animal God created shows his superior intelligence. He made a tragic choice, however, against God's life support system when he chose in favor of the tree of knowledge of good and evil and against the tree of life. The brilliant career was ended.

God makes it a point to clarify that Adam acted with clear understanding of the consequences (1 Timothy 2:14). What an epitaph has been affixed to Adam's posterity through centuries of time:

"Wherefore as by one man sin entered into the world and death by sin; and so death passed upon all men, for that all have sinned" (Romans 5:12).

Adam's sin was charged to all mankind. The word "imputed" in verse 13 means "charged." Even the people living between the times of Adam and Moses, before there was a law, died because of the sin of Adam. More than a hundred years ago, Charles Simeon of Cambridge commented on our oneness with Adam: "How deep and unsearchable are the ways of God! That even our first parent should be constituted a federal head to his posterity, so that they should stand or fall in him, is in itself a stupendous mystery."

Simeon went on to say that if each of us were asked whether he should be judged in Adam or in himself, the thinking person would choose to be judged in Adam. For Adam lived in very favorable circumstances and faced only one temptation. We live in unfavorable circumstances and face innumerable temptations. Adam functioned with the brilliance of a mind freshly created. Our minds are dulled and our judgments impaired from the wear and tear of sin. There can be no doubt that if Adam sinned in his favorable circumstances, how much more likely that we would do even worse. In the same circumstances today we would fall faster and farther, if that is possible. So before blaming Adam unfairly, remember that you have a more favorable standing in him than if you stood on your own record.

Right at this point many people have gagged on the truth of God's word and rejected it. Donald Grey Barnhouse points out, "The basic hatred of man is against God Himself; but unable to attack directly, men attack the truths at the edges of Christian doctrine and hope thus to undermine the whole." Barnhouse quotes the former Oxford agnostic, C. S. Lewis, who was converted to Jesus Christ. C. S. Lewis described this method in his introduction to J. B. Phillips' *Letters to Young Churches*, applying it to the attack on the works of the Apostle Paul:

In the earlier history of every rebellion there is a stage at which you do not yet attack the King in person. You say, "The King is all right. It is his Ministers who are wrong. They misrepresent him and corrupt all his plans which, I'm sure, are good plans if only the Ministers would let them take effect." And the first victory consists in beheading a few Ministers; only at a later stage do you go on and behead the King himself.

Now turn your attention to the MUCH MORE of the second Adam.

What One Man Did to Right the Wrong

Although the first Adam and the second Adam, Jesus Christ, have similar qualities, they are, for the most part, actually incomparable. Adam was a figure of Christ but became a broken figure.

Adam had a brilliant but brief career.
Christ had a brief but brilliant career.
From the side of Adam came a bride, one person.
From the wounded side of Christ came a bride, multitudes making up the church.
In his fall, Adam took his bride with him to sin's bondage.
In His victory, Christ is taking His bride with Him to life's liberty.

In the second Adam there is MUCH MORE! "... *much more the grace of God, and the gift by grace, which is by one man, Jesus Christ, hath abounded unto man*" (Romans 5:15b). The defeat of Adam pales before the victory of Jesus Christ. Just as light has the power to dispel darkness, so Christ's power always has the preeminence over Adam's power. The gift of grace in Jesus Christ can undo what Adam has done. But Adam can never undo what Christ has done. And so we sing:

"Death cannot keep his prey,
 Jesus, my Saviour;
He tore the bars away,
 Jesus, my Lord.
Up from the grave He arose,
 With a mighty triumph o'er His foes;

He arose a victor from the dark domain,
And He lives forever with His saints to reign!
He arose! He arose!
Hallelujah! Christ Arose!"

The comments of Dr. Barnhouse concerning Christ's uncontestable victory are a fitting conclusion to this discussion of His abounding grace:

> ... The Lord Jesus Christ is the eternal God. What He has promised He is able to perform (Romans 4:21). What He has planned He will surely bring to pass. He has never started anything that He will not finish; when He begins a good work in us, He will keep on perfecting it until the day of His return (Philippians 1:6). All power is His (Matthew 28:18). His name is not the Alpha and the Beta; His name is the Alpha and the Omega, the beginning and the ending (Revelation 1:8). He is not the Lord of the nearly or the almost; He is the Lord of the MUCH MORE.

3. The MUCH MORE of His Conquering Reign

In the first part of verse 17, the reign of death is reviewed, but in the MUCH MORE of the verse, the reigning rights to life are revealed in Christ Jesus. *"For if by one man's offense death reigned by one; much more they which receive abundance of grace and of the gift of righteousness shall reign in life by one, Jesus Christ"* (Romans 5:17). Death's reign was uncontested until Jesus' reign began. The longest and blackest shadow in history was cast by death. Sooner or later every individual and every civilization has moved under its ominous darkness.

Now a new King has come to reign! In Him we reign in life instead of living in the shadow of death. Even when we walk into the valley of the shadow of death we will fear no evil, for this reigning King is with us. The abundance of grace and the benefits of righteousness in Him enable us to enjoy a reigning life style, even as He is seated *"Far above all principality, and power, and might, and dominion, and every name that is named, not only in this world, but also in that which is to come:"* we have been *"made [to] sit together in the heavenly places in Christ Jesus"* (Ephesians 1:21, 2:6). We are seated to reign as He is reigning. His life is our life; His power is our power. His victory is our victory, SO WE CAN REIGN IN LIFE. Hallelujah! Get out from under the pile of circumstances and take your reserved seat on the spiritual fifty-yard line to reign in life. No wonder Charles Wesley sang:

> "He breaks the power of reigning sin,
>   He sets the prisoner free;
> His blood can make the foulest clean,
>   His blood availed for me."

4. The MUCH MORE of His Abounding Righteousness

> His Life within us,
> His Grace for us,
> His Reign with us . . . produce
> His Righteousness through us.

God is interested only in *one* life style—the life style of righteousness. Amazing grace results in abounding righteousness. Grace is never a license for sin but the power for obtaining victory over it. Revival always brings us to God's MUCH MORE of abounding grace: *"But where sin abounded, grace did much more abound: That as sin hath reigned unto death, even so might grace reign through righteousness unto eternal life by Jesus Christ our Lord"* (Romans 5:20b-21). God's supply of grace sown liberally in a life always produces righteousness. When the psalmist sought for revival, he saw righteousness as its primary fruit:

> *wilt thou not revive us again that thy people may rejoice in thee? Mercy and truth are met together; righteousness and peace have kissed each other. . . . righteousness shall look down from heaven. . . . righteousness shall go before him, and shall set us in the way of his steps* (Psalm 85:6, 10, 11b, 13).

When an astronaut goes to the moon he always

carries a life support system with him which, of course, includes oxygen tanks. Every step taken on the moon requires oxygen from earth's support system. The astronaut breathes the atmosphere of earth while walking in the surroundings of the moon. Every accomplishment in outer space has required moving earth's atmosphere to outer space. For righteousness to be exhibited in this earth, HEAVEN'S SUPPORT SYSTEM MUST BE MOVED INTO US. The Christian breathes the atmosphere of heaven while walking in the surroundings of this earth. Abounding grace released in us through Jesus Christ results in a walk that is righteous on this earth.

THE POSITION OF EVERY CHRISTIAN

Romans 6:1–16

The Obituary Column of the Bible is found in Romans chapter six. The identity of every Christian can be found here. It was shocking but relieving to discover my name listed among the deceased one day over ten years ago. Many Christians are dead and don't know it and that's why, though dead, they can't show it.

"What God Wants You to Know" would be a perfect title for the sixth chapter of Romans. In this chapter, four verses—3, 6, 9, and 16—announce what we are to know to enjoy the liberty of the Christ-life. These four verses disclose the major message of the chapter, so our study will concentrate on them.

THE IMPORTANCE OF KNOWING WHEN YOU DIED

Verse 3 declares that when you were baptized into Christ you were put to death. Our baptism into Jesus Christ is a spiritual baptism. The baptizer is the Holy Spirit. His purpose is to immerse us into all that Christ is.

In a day of renewed emphasis on the Holy Spirit, there is a great deal of misusage of the term "baptism of the Holy Spirit." The Bible uses the term "baptism of the Holy Spirit" as pre-Pente-costal (before the day of Pentecost) terminology. The post-Pentecostal (after the day of Pentecost) terminology is the "filling of the Spirit," with two exceptions in the book of Acts. In these two in-stances the gospel was being preached for the first time in a certain place, and the pattern of the day of Pentecost was repeated. On the day of Pente-cost the Holy Spirit baptized all who already knew Christ and all who were then receiving Christ as Lord and Savior. From that day on He has taken everyone coming to Christ through three steps: (1) He convicts us of sin so we know why we need Christ (John 16:18-11); (2) He introduces us to Christ so we know definitely who He is (1 Corinthians 12:3); (3) He baptizes us into Christ so we now have assurance of our salvation (Gala-tians 3:26-27).

As L. E. Maxwell says in his book BORN CRUCI-FIED, we were born dead. Our spiritual birth and spiritual baptism occur simultaneously. We are born into the family of God and baptized into Christ in one and the same act of the Holy Spirit.

THE IMPORTANCE OF KNOWING WHERE YOU DIED

"Know ye not, that so many of us as were bap-tized into Jesus Christ were baptized into his death?" (Romans 6:3). The moment we were baptized into Jesus Christ, we were baptized into

His death. Just as we have seen that we were charged with Adam's sin, so we see now that Christ's death was charged to us also. When He died, we died. Thus when we are placed in Christ, we are placed in the position of His death. The clearest picture of how a holy God can have an association with sinful flesh like you and me is found in the study of the Tabernacle. In considering that fifty chapters of the Bible deal with that subject compared to two chapters on the account of the creation, you see the weighty importance ascribed to the Tabernacle account.

From that first visual display of God in the Tabernacle through the years of worship in the temple built by Solomon, God was approached through the blood offering of animals put to death at the altar. Upon entering the outer court, the priest (a picture of the Christian today) would encounter the brazen altar first. The Hebrews called it the "killing place." There the animal whose blood had been spilled was placed on the altar to be consumed. Only by passing the station of death could the priest go on to the brass laver, then enter the Holy Place, and finally move on to the Holy of Holies where the presence of God himself resided between the cherubims above the mercy seat.

That physical picture in the Old Testament is a spiritual principle in the New Testament. Our first encounter with Christ also brings us to death. We cannot go on to further fellowship with God without passing through death. Jesus said, *"If any man will come after me, let him deny himself and take up his cross daily, and follow me"* (Luke 9:23).

When I was in Taiwan in 1970, I ministered in the south coastal city of Kaohsiung for a week. At the end of the crusade, my missionary host, Dr. Hogue, asked if I'd enjoy a trip to the mountains since I had a day free before going to the next crusade in Tinan. When I told him of my great enjoyment of mountains anywhere, we were off. After a few hours of driving in the land known as the "beautiful island" (Formosa), we began climbing the foothills at the base of the mountain range that stretches right up the island. The majestic mountains were just ahead. Already the cool breezes from those higher elevations were blowing gently on us and furnishing a welcome reprieve from the sweltering heat of the subtropical climate of Taiwan. Around the next turn of the road we encountered a barricade and a sign announcing that the road was closed except to those with proper credentials. Dr. Hogue said we could proceed no further. Sensing my disappointment, he explained that the Nationalist government had learned at a very high cost on the mainland of China never to let the enemy get into the mountains. So to keep from repeating that tragic lesson, the mountains of Taiwan were a restricted area, open only to people with certified credentials affirming their loyalty to the government. Only people who could be trusted were permitted to enjoy the highlands. Since Dr. Hogue's mountain pass had just expired, we could go no further.

We too must have a "mountain pass" to go further with the Lord. That pass is the credentials of the cross of Christ. By our passing through death, the self-life is put to death, and we then can be trusted in the highlands of spiritual reality.

THE IMPORTANCE OF KNOWING WHY YOU DIED

A problem still present today was dealt with by Paul in verses 1 and 2 of chapter six. "*What shall we say then? Shall we continue in sin, that grace may abound? God forbid. How shall we that are dead to sin, live any longer therein?*" Some had concluded that since grace is given because sin demands it, and since grace is so wonderful, then why not sin more and thus guarantee a greater supply of grace? Paul concluded it to be inconceivable that anyone who is dead to sin can live any longer in it. Because we were placed in Christ's death and should act like it, we have been placed in His resurrected life and should act like it, Paul argues in verse 5. Then he points again to what we are to know: "*Knowing this, that our old man is crucified with him, that the body of sin might be destroyed, that henceforth we should not serve sin*" (Romans 6:6). Verse 7 lets us know why it's to our advantage to die. ". . . *he that is dead is freed from sin.*"

Our old sin nature (the old man) was pronounced dead when Christ died just as much as our sins were pronounced forgiven or paid for. 1 John 2:2 reveals: *"And he is the propitiation for our sins, and not for ours only, but also for the sins of the whole world."* Every person's sins were paid for as Christ died. That explains why people don't go to hell because of their sins, but because of their unbelief or refusal of Christ (John 3:18).

Two colossal things were done for us at the cross: (1) Jesus shed His blood to cleanse us from sin, and (2) He shared His cross to crucify the sinner. Most people have been taught only the first aspect of Christ's work at the cross.

The minute we awake in the brand new world of being saved, we discover that a very old problem has followed us there—the nagging and exasperating problem of sin. We can still sin. Some difference has occurred in our lives, to be sure, as pointed out in chapter one. We see these differences in us but discover we are not totally changed. Hudson Taylor was right when he said, "The Christian Life is Not a Changed Life, but an Exchanged Life." The cross of Christ became God's exchange station where the old nature dies and Christ's life rules.

Some of the most frustrated people on the face of the earth (with earth's face, not heaven's, shining through them) are Christians trying to live without the power of Christ to overcome sin. Rededication has followed rededication until they usually have sent several well-worn "rededicators" to the scrap heap. It is interesting that the concept of rededication was invented when mass evangelism produced Christians coming to make commitments. Rededication is not called for in the Bible, but crucifixion is. Scores of conscientious Christians have been left only half way to victory when they "rededicated." They came conscientiously to confess their sins and "live for Christ." They missed the fact that Christ wanted to live for them, so they gave Him their sins but that's all. Turning in our sins is not enough: we must turn in the sinner also. In rededication, most people stop short of turning in the sinner, the real problem, and accepting God's perfect solution to the conflict as they accept their death with Christ.

Let me illustrate how we stop short of claiming the real victory of Christ. Suppose your neighbor rushes into your house right now without even knocking, shouting that another distant neighbor, Barney Burns, has lost his mind and has a blow torch in his hand, has already set two houses on fire, and is applying the blow torch to her house right then. The neighbor, nearing hysteria, shouts to you to call for help and races on down the block to warm other neighbors. What would you do—call the fire department or police department? Since there are two houses already blazing and another catching fire by now, your first thought will probably be to call the fire department. So you do and more excitement follows. Red fire trucks with red lights flashing and sirens wailing converge on the scene. Trained men start filling the street with fire hoses. Now before you breathe a sign of relief, let me point out that although the fires can probably be stopped eventually, that's not your problem. In the meantime, Barney Burns can set ten more houses on fire. The problem is not the fire; the problem is the guy with the blow torch. You need the police department to capture the arsonist even more than the fire department to put out the fire. Ideally, of course, you need both. The fire can then be extinguished and the police can capture the real culprit.

Jesus did both for us at the cross. He shed His blood to put out the fires of sin already started. He shared His cross to capture the sinner. So we can turn in our sins and the sinner. In his little booklet *If It Die*, McCall Barbour relates so well why we must die:

> A life of overcoming, an ever victorious life, a life of ceaseless praise! How desirable! How needful! What is it that hinders this blessed experience and possession? Surely it can be nothing and none other than "Self." "Self," says William Law, "is not only the seat and habitation, but the very life of sin." The works of the devil are all wrought in self; it is his peculiar workshop. "Self" is the obstacle. Therefore Self must be removed if the desired blessing is

to be experienced and possessed. "Self" must be put out of the way. But how? IT MUST DIE!

THE IMPORTANCE OF KNOWING HOW YOU DIED

Know How God Counts

The answers to the questions of "how you died" and "how to die" are in Romans 6:9-11: *"Knowing that Christ being raised from the dead dieth no more; death hath no more dominion over him. For in that he died, he died unto sin once: but in that he liveth, he liveth unto God. Likewise reckon ye also yourselves to be dead indeed unto sin, but alive unto God through Jesus Christ our Lord."*

What was done as one final completing act by the Lord Jesus we are now privileged to reckon upon. Just as we have realized our justification, sanctification, and glorification by allowing Christ to do it for us, even so must dying to self be done for us by the Lord Jesus. Self-crucifixion is no more valid than self-justification, self-sanctification, or self-glorification.

Dr. C. L. Culpepper, who was among the company of Christians privileged to see the Shantung revival in China, tells of his own efforts to crucify himself. He vividly describes nailing himself limb by limb to the cross. But then he could never get the hand with the hammer nailed down. Each time he pulled the already crucified hand loose and grasped the hammer to nail up the active hand, he found he still had a loose hand holding the hammer.

No, we do not crucify ourselves. Since we died with Christ, we don't have to. We reckon death a reality now. The word reckon (*logizomai*) can be translated "number," "count," "impute," "account," "estimate." It is an accountant's term that implies mathematical accounting. In God's system of bookkeeping you are counted dead! You can count on being dead because you are!

Counting That Counts

If you count on being dead, what will you count on yourself for? Nothing, obviously! As you count on yourself for nothing you are counting on yourself for exactly what God is counting on you for—nothing! "*. . . ye are dead, and your life is hid with Christ in God*" (Colossians 3:3). Jesus said, "*. . . without me you can do nothing*" (John 15:5b). Most people count on being weak. They say, "I am weak; pray for me." A weak person can do something. Not much, maybe, but something. If you count on yourself to be weak, you are still counting on yourself a little. If you count on being dead, you are counting on yourself for nothing. Who you count on determines your victory or your defeat. The self-life is a loser; the Christ-life is a winner! Jess Moody is right—"You can't lose for winning" when you count on Christ.

Keep on Counting

Don't stop counting too soon. We must also count on being made alive unto God through Jesus Christ. Counting on life is just as important as counting on death. Jesus counted on death all His life. Yet when He came to die He was counting on life. In essence He said to sorrowing disciples, "I'll see you later."

Some have objected very strongly to the "death to self" concept. They interpret it as producing an annihilation of self resulting in a passive, vegetable personality resembling a wet dish rag more than a dynamic human personality. By counting on being dead to sin and alive to God, however, we are really experiencing the termination of the old life and the realization of a new life. A new self now emerges—a self worthy of acceptance. I was asked in a university setting a few years ago how I harmonized the death of self with the admonishing of Jesus in Mark 12:13 to love ourselves. It's easy. I know better than anyone else the old self in me. Take it from me—he can't be loved. That fraudulent character isn't lovable. I believe that's why— as Mininger, the famous psychiatrist of Topeka, Kansas, has pointed out—there is a suicidal instinct in all of us. It is with ease, though, that I can love the new self as Christ becomes my life. I can hold my head up in the best of company.

Late in 1969, a group of us who were conducting crusades in India had an audience with Madam Indira Gandhi. I was quite confident meeting the Prime Minister of India, who leads one sixth of the world's population. As a child of the King, I have the right to call on the head of state of any country. I have no problem loving myself now.

Counting Now

Paul's timetable for counting was NOW. He testified, "*I am crucified with Christ: nevertheless I live: yet not I, but Christ liveth in me: and the life which I now live in the flesh I live by the faith of the Son of God, who loved me, and gave himself for me*" (Galatians 2:20). Paul had learned the secret of living now. Most people live either victimized by the past or pressurized by the future. God's time is NOW. Living one now at a time is the secret to victory in Christ. Yesterday's victories or defeats don't count. Tomorrow will arrive as today—so live now.

The principle of aerodynamics will serve to illustrate the timetable of victorious counting. Though the principle of aerodynamics is a proven principle, it's amazing how skeptical many people are of flying in an airplane. Insurance companies sell "fat" policies in air terminals because people distrust aerodynamics. Though flying is some thirteen times safer per mile traveled than highway driving, service stations don't offer travel insurance for people in a car because we trust the more familiar automobile.

When you count on being dead and count on being alive unto God you find yourself flying faster than the speed of self, and sin is left behind. The minute you stop counting on your position in Christ, you start falling. Falling won't hurt, but the world gets in your way and you hit spiritual bottom. You wake up with sin (your unwelcome companion) licking you in the face like a shaggy stray dog. It has caught up to you again.

What next? Right then and there you turn in your sin and yourself, the sinner, and count on Christ again. You're right back in the position to go on LIVING NOW!

THE IMPORTANCE OF KNOWING WHAT YOU DIED TO

The last verse in this course of KNOWING is verse 16 of chapter 6: "*Know ye not, that to whom ye yield yourselves servants to obey, his servants ye are to whom ye obey; whether of sin unto death, or of obedience unto righteousness?*"

What have we died to in Christ? We have died to disobedience and its associates. In Christ we live to obedience and its benefits. Our yieldedness determines which column we fall into.

DISOBEDIENCE:	OBEDIENCE:
Sin, vs. 17	God's teaching (doctrine) vs. 17
Infirmity of the flesh, vs. 19	Righteousness, vs. 18
Uncleanness, vs. 19	Holiness, vs. 19
Iniquity, vs. 19	Fruitfulness, vs. 22
DEATH IS THE PAYOFF, vs. 23.	*ETERNAL LIFE AS A GIFT FROM JESUS CHRIST*, vs. 23.

Our wills are to be consistently exercised in favor of obedience to Christ. Some people erroneously conclude that if they are dead and can't do it, and Christ is alive and can do it, they are to be passive and do nothing. Not so! We are to be participants.

The illustration of Ian Thomas about pushing the car instead of enjoying it will serve well. Many Christians are like a person owning a powerful automobile, who instead of riding in the car and enjoying it feel obligated to push it. Once they discover the car was designed to be ridden in and not pushed, they must choose their position carefully. Since the car has more than ample power and accessories, it must be driven. So they must occupy the front seat, not the back, and make available their senses, driving ability, and experience to the car. The car furnishes the power and forward motion, and they will be either a participant or a statistic. Yieldedness is never passive but always active. So in the future, take your position in Christ, yield to His power, and please obey all traffic signals!

THE PROVOCATION OF EVERY CHRISTIAN

Romans 7:1–6

TWO QUESTIONS

The question of where to place Romans seven in Paul's experience with Christ has been debated for years. Some have contended that this is an account of Paul's pre-conversion experience. Others have said it was his post-conversion experience. Still others have taken the position that it was a combination of both. I believe it is a resumé of his life as a Christian, for the following reasons:

1. In verse 22 he relates, *"I delight in the law of God after the inward man."* The "inward man" in Scripture refers most of the time to the new nature, Christ in us. In the first three chapters of Romans, Paul declares that no person without Christ "delights in the law of God," "desires good," or "desires righteousness." The word "delight" (*sumedomai*) is a strong word denoting intense desire. Since "no good thing" dwells in the flesh (vs. 18), and Paul has a strong delight in the law of God and thus for good, I must conclude he is writing as a Christian.

2. A parallel account to Romans 7 is found in Galatians 5. The Galatians passage obviously concerns Christians. *"Walk in the Spirit, and ye*

shall not fulfill the lust of the flesh. For the flesh lusteth against the Spirit and the Spirit against the flesh: and these are contrary the one to the other: so that ye cannot do the things that ye would" (Galatians 5:16-17). While operating out of the resources of the flesh we can't do what we would. That is exactly Paul's testimony in Romans 7:19: "*For good that I would I do not: but the evil which I would not, that I do.*" Since Romans seven and Galatians five are parallel problems and Galatians five is written to Christians, I must conclude that Romans seven is written about a Christian.

3. The chronological sequence in which Romans seven falls also provides evidence that it is Paul's experience as a Christian. The sin problem is covered in chapters one and two; God's redemptive solution is reviewed in chapters three and four. Chapter five, where we began this study, is a transition introducing the Christian life. Since seven appears in the heart of the survey of Christian living, I must conclude again that it concerns the Christian life.

4. My experience as a Christian is identical to Paul's recorded here. My life story as a Christian was told here before I ever lived to write it. While Scripture is never the servant of experience but vice versa, our experiences can serve to make us aware of, if not verify, scriptural principles. From experiential evidence, I reason again it is a treatment of the Christian life.

In light of the preceding reasoning, a second question arises that needs answering. After describing our position in Christ that enables us to claim Christ's life as ours in chapter six, how can Paul not describe his life of defeat in chapter seven? The answer is found in understanding the difference between positional and conditional truth. Because positional truth and conditional truth do not always link arms and progress together as companions, we see at least three patterns of progression in the Christian life: (1) Experience runs ahead of understanding; (2) understanding and experience develop together and proceed side by side; (3) understanding proceeds and experience lags behind.

It is unusual for a person's experience to exceed his understanding, though occasionally it does happen. Ideally, understanding and experience would keep step together. But the pattern of progress for most people is for understanding to outdistance experience; then experience catches up later. Thus, our position provisionally and our condition experientially are two different things. Paul knew his position in Romans six but that was not his condition in Romans seven. In Romans eight his condition caught up with his position.

Positionally, I literally live at 910 Grace Avenue in West Plains, Missouri. It's wonderful to live on Grace Avenue. Living on God's supply (Grace) means that my needs are met before they arise. Figuratively, I once lived at the corner of

Self-Effort Boulevard and Self-Sufficiency Lane. That was a bad neighborhood. Now literally and figuratively, I live on Grace Avenue. That's my position provisionally. At any time, though, I can go home, for that's my rightful position. Paul was away from his rightful position in Romans seven, but returned home in chapter eight.

A PROVOKING MARRIAGE VS. A PERFECT MARRIAGE

The Unhappy Marriage

At first glance Paul appears to be discussing marriage and divorce in Romans 7:1-6. It becomes apparent, however, that he is not, but is using it as an analogy of the Christian life. He makes his point in verse 4: *"Wherefore, my brethren, ye also are become dead to the law by the body of Christ, that ye should be married to another, even to him who is raised from the dead."*

Allow me to illustrate Paul's analogy with another in contemporary terms. Imagine a fine young lady meeting a fine young all-American boy. They begin dating and fall in love. When he pops the question "Wilt thou?" she promptly "wilts." They marry, assuming what everyone assumes at marriage—they have found a perfect companion. To her amazement, she discovers her assumption is correct. Her husband is perfect. There is not a fault or flaw to be found. He is a paragon of excellence. Because the husband is perfect, everything he does is excellent. As a business man he has the astuteness of a Wall Street tycoon. When she handles finances, she always has more "month than money." He not only enjoys a good home, but can keep it better than she. When she keeps house she has dirt left over at the end of every rug. Not only is he a connoisseur of good food; he can cook with skills that would make the Galloping Gourmet envious. Her cooking at best is blah. In social events he is poised and at ease; conversant on any subject, he seems to know how to say the right thing to everyone. Her "tang gets tonguled" and since she is "backward," she says things backwards.

Living with a perfectionist whom she admires causes her to try to her utmost to join her husband in achieving excellence. She attends every housekeeping course she can. She studies how to win friends and influence people. Instead of her achieving, her house goes unkept while she is learning to keep house, and she influences people to win other friends. Discouragement grows close to despair as she realizes she can never achieve the goal of perfection. As she awakens to the dismal prospect of another day she mutters, "Good Lord, it's morning," instead of "Good morning, Lord!" and heads for the kitchen. Placing what could reasonably be called breakfast on the table, she sees her husband coming in from completing a repair job on the house. He's bright-eyed, enthusiastic, and abounding with energy. His very appearance is threatening to her. As she sits across the breakfast table from him in the "dark brown" state of depression she concludes, "I wish we weren't married. If we weren't married, then I could find a husband like me and we could live together compatibly and enjoyably." Checking herself momentarily with "Don't think this so early in the morning," her thoughts resume: "How could we not be married?" Telling herself not to think about it, she concludes that "if he could die painlessly of a heart attack, then I could marry another and be happy." That possibility, though a fantasy, brings a temporary reprieve. Then two days later she observes him reading a book titled *The Royal Canadian Air Force Manual on Physical Fitness*. Her hopes crash as she watches him begin a program of exercise that results in his growing healthier every day. Despair grips her. She cries out, "I just wish I could . . . die. Die! Why didn't I see it before? I've expected the wrong person to die. If I die then I can be married to another," she concludes.

Now that long story is worth the time and printed space we've used, if you see that we too must die to be "*married to another even to him who is raised from the dead*," Jesus Christ.

The Fruit of an Unhappy Marriage

Every Christian lives at one of two places, either Sinai or Calvary; and every Christian has one of two husbands. The Christian lives either at Sinai married to the law, or at Calvary married to Christ. When we meet Christ, we meet Him where God meets sinners—at Calvary. But without realizing how, when, or where, we gradually gravitate to Sinai for a residency. There we become the "do it yourselfer" in residence. Our companion is the law, a perfectionist. We admire him and try to please him, but our performance is inferior. We grow more and more weary, "Doing more in seventy-four," "Looking alive in seventy-five," and "Getting out of our fix with the spirit of 76." Courses on soul-winning-made-easy and how-to-be-happy-while-trying leave us uneasy soul winners and unhappy people while trying to be happy.

At this stage hundreds of Christians have "thrown in the towel," given up, and walked out of churches never to come back. Annually in America twenty thousand men leave the ministry in defeat and frustration having graduated from Sinai's law school. I can understand their frustration. There was a time in my own life when I would have thrown in the towel but the Lord graciously concealed from me the "throw in the towel" container. In addition to the high casualty rate among ministers, there are so many spiritual casualties among laymen that Southern Baptists alone have three and one half million of these missing persons.

No one (I think) intends to build and settle

down at Sinai, so how do we accomplish it? Traditions offer us poor alternatives to God's plan of looking to Christ plus nothing, minus nothing. We build laws out of traditions, marry them, and live unhappily ever after. Tragically these sacred cows are not necessarily holy cows.

A GUIDE FOR LOCATING YOURSELF

Sinai	RESIDENCE	Calvary
The Law	MARRIAGE	Christ
Doing	ACTIVITY	Claiming What's Done
Trying	ATTITUDE	Trusting
Routine	EXPERIENCE	Romance
Duty	SERVICE	Delight

The Happy Marriage

In death (positional) the intolerable relationship with the law is broken. We are free, free to enjoy a relationship with Christ. We discover in our relationship to Christ that He is no less perfect than the law, nor does He expect less of us. Instead of demanding of us, He offers Himself as the indwelling adequacy for accomplishing the demands made on us. Dr. Stephen Olford, preacher with few peers, who has served as spiritual advisor to Billy Graham through the years, has a motto for his life: "Every demand made upon my life is made on the life of Jesus Christ in me."

The law demands, "Read your Bible." You try

and it's a wooden book with wooden words for a seemingly wooden head.

Christ says, "Trust Me as you read your Bible and let My mind be in you to give you the desire to read, enjoyment during the experience, and understanding of what you have read."

The law demands, "Pray." You try with short prayers, long prayers, verbal prayers, silent prayers, formal prayers, informal prayers, but praying is a meaningless monologue.

Christ says, "Trust me and pray and I will direct you in how to pray, what to pray for. Don't try to impress Me; let Me impress you. In My authority I'll grant the agreements we reach in prayer."

The law says, "Witness." You try to show up on visitation night scared to death, fearing you may draw the name of a Jewish Rabbi. You're disappointed to find people at home, but relieved it's not a Jewish Rabbi. Finally you blurt out, "You don't want to be a Christian do you?" They don't, and you leave seeing yourself a failure.

Christ says, "Trust Me, even if it's a Jewish Rabbi. I've talked to many. I'll give you love and wisdom. Even if they refuse Me, you're not a failure; for I will continue to appeal to them through you and others."

Dr. Jack Johnson, dynamic pastor of First Southern Baptist Church in El Monte, California, and present President of the California State Convention, told me of the day he was about to be one of Sinai's casualties. He was prepared to leave the ministry and had already been accepted by the University of Oklahoma in his home state to study law. Then a friend recommended Jack Taylor's book *The Key to Triumphant Living* to him. As Jack Johnson read *The Key* he saw the way to leave the frustrations of relating to the law and made his way to victory in Christ at Calvary. Instead of leaving the ministry, he wears a P.O.W. bracelet which means to him PRISONER OF WOE. *"Woe is unto me, if I preach not the gospel!"* (1 Cor. 9:16b). It is gratifying today to see thousands of people "living happily ever after," married to Christ.

"Free from the law, O happy condition
　　Jesus hath died, and there is remission
Cursed by the law and bruised by the fall
　　Grace hath redeemed us once for all.

'Children of God,' O glorious calling
　　Surely His grace will keep us from falling
Passing from death to life at His call
　　Blessed Salvation once for all."

The Fruit of Happy Marriage

The purpose of BEING MARRIED TO ANOTHER, to Christ WHO WAS RAISED FROM THE DEAD, is to BRING FORTH FRUIT UNTO GOD. It has been said "the fruit of a Christian is another Christian." Indirectly this may be so, but the fruit of a Christian directly is the fruit of the Spirit. *"But the fruit of the Spirit is love, joy, peace, longsuffering, gentleness, goodness, faith, meekness, temperance"* (Galatians 5:22-23a). In Australia there is a fruit similar to our orange, yet different in that the sections have different flavors and even different textures. The fruit of the Spirit is one fruit, but seven qualities exist in it. We are to exhibit this luscious fruit produced by the Holy Spirit through abiding fully in Christ. He is the vine and we are the branches. We abide and He produces. Each abiding Christian is a fruit-stand Christian. When people encounter the fruit-stand Christian, they can pick up the fruit they need from the love, joy, peace, patience, gentleness, goodness, faith, meekness, and temperance on display.

THE PROBLEM OF EVERY CHRISTIAN

Romans 7:7–25

THE PROBLEM PERSONIFIED

The Bible has always been its best commentary. A careful look at two people closely associated with Christ will illustrate the differences of living the "law life" and the Christ-life introduced in the last chapter. Christ's visit in the home of Mary and Martha personifies this difference perfectly. The account is in Luke 10:38-42.

When it was learned that Jesus was coming, Martha's response was "Think of all the things I must do." Mary's response was "Think of all the things Jesus will do." Already conditioned to the law of "doing" when Jesus arrived, Martha responded to the age-old motto "Do something even if it's wrong." Assuming the thing to do was to get a meal, she started one. We don't know what she prepared, but it was probably a stew, for she was certainly in one. "Stewing" away in her stew, she remembered that the better the stew, the more you have in it. Not wanting to be the only ingredient in her stew she went to Jesus and said, *"Lord, dost thou not care that my sister hath left me to serve alone? bid her, therefore, that she help me"* (vs. 40). (People who are in a stew are never content to "abide alone.") Jesus said, *"Martha, Martha, thou art careful and troubled about many things: But one thing is needful and Mary hath chosen that good part"* (vs. 41-42). Mary had found the secret of abiding in Christ. Instead of doing something for Him, she sat at His feet receiving all He could do for her.

Scriptural alteration has been a common practice for years—that is, fitting the Scripture to our practice. This event in Christ's life, as well as Romans seven, has sometimes been more than slightly altered. Romans has become the Fifth Amendment for Christians. It is the "proof text" for defeat. Reasoning with the same mentality "that since the King James was good enough for Paul, it's good enough for me," the person asks, "Didn't Paul say that the thing I want to do I don't do, and the things I don't want to do I am always doing?" When you agree he did, the person concludes with great satisfaction, "If that's good enough for Paul, it's good enough for me." The fact is, it was not good enough for Paul, as we will see, for he cried out, *"O, wretched man that I am, who shall deliver me from the body of this death?"* (vs. 24).

Alterations have also been made on Martha's problem so it will fit us more comfortably. People say, "Well, the church needs Marthas and Marys. Martha is a pragmatist who gets the practical things done. A mystic like Mary is O.K., but common sense will tell you we can't pray, study, and witness all the time." Of course men have the same temperaments. There are as many Martins as Marthas and Marions as Marys in the church today. Do we really need Marthas and Martins in the church? Is it essential that we have people in a stew getting as many others in their stew as they can? Would a "de-Marthaized" church cease to function?

I am more interested in Jesus' evaluation than anyone else's. He said, ". . . *one thing is needful: and Mary hath chosen that good part, which shall not be taken away from her*" (Luke 10:42). I don't think He considered Martha's stew necessary. We have all been conditioned to think that Jesus needed Martha's best that day. But did He?

Let's see if He needed her best on other occasions. Look at fifteen to twenty-five thousand people gathered in a beautiful setting for dining, a hillside overlooking the Sea of Galilee. Everything was perfect, except that the only food available was five crusty loaves and two small, salty fishes. People were fainting from hunger, and Philip was trying to figure out how to raise or borrow the needed money to buy food. Andrew had gotten the "starter" but concluded, "What's that among so many?" In all this, can't you see Jesus pacing nervously, wringing His hands, muttering, "Oh, if only a committee could be formed to get Martha here with her portable kitchen, we could feed this crowd?" No, you can't see Jesus in that role, for He didn't need Martha that day. He broke and blessed five loaves and two fishes. The food had to be broken to make way for Himself. It had to be blessed so that He Himself could make it adequate. His blessing means He is available and adequate. So, not needing Philip's attempt to borrow money, or Martha's culinary skills, He took fifteen to twenty-five thousand people to lunch and left the disciples with twelve baskets full of surplus food.

Did He need Martha's lunch at Bethany that day? No! Had Martha not had her stew, He might have snapped a cookie wafer left from tea that morning, broken it to add Himself, blessed it to be Himself, and served the most memorable meal ever. But He didn't because Martha already had a stew. Ever wonder why the Lord doesn't do more for us? Could it be we are so busy doing it ourselves, we don't give Him a chance?

Or Jesus might have said to Mary, "Before we take up another principle, best that you fix lunch. Remember when 'Saved-way' had the sale on and you stocked up on canned goods? Just start heating some food and I'll talk some more while it's preparing." Mary, not Martha, would have gone to the kitchen. She would have fixed a wholesome meal under Christ's direction, not a stew. Many people have concluded that a Mary temperament is a "do nothing" person who is so "heavenly-minded that she is of no earthly good." That's not so at all. Mary will get more done in the kitchen than Martha, because Martha will probably go to bed with a migraine headache from tension, or be so tired from the expenditure of nervous energy, she can't keep going.

True spirituality is not ignoring the tasks that need to be done, however. Catherine Marshall points out that if a lady is reading her books with housework piled up, believing she's more spiritual by reading, she ought to do her housework first, then allot the time left to read the book. True spirituality includes giving attention to the practical and the capacity to function at the maximum while doing our routine tasks. There must be a balance of both.

THE PROBLEM DISCOVERED
(Find the Facts)

Locating the problem that produced the provocation described in the preceding chapter is our next assignment. The question immediately asked is IS THE LAW SIN? Then the answer, GOD FORBID. Could the law have been the problem in some way? Let's look at scriptural facts and reach a conclusion.

Fact No. 1. The law showed us sin, *"I had not known sin, but by the law"* (vs. 7a). The law does not produce sin; it simply points it out—just as light does not clutter a room, but when lit reveals the clutter that's already there.

Fact No. 2. The law reveals the root of sin. *"I had not known lust, except the law had said, Thou shalt not covet"* (vs. 7b). Francis Schaeffer says that the essence of all sin is coveting. Though Paul stood before the law blameless through nine counts, when the law said, *"Thou shalt not covet,"* he was convicted. All sin flows from the spring of our desires or from coveting. We may do the right thing but not actually want to. We may refuse the wrong thing, yet really desire it in our hearts.

Fact No. 3. The law incites our sin nature. When the commandment came, all manner of sin occurred and BUT WHEN THE COMMANDMENT CAME, sin revived. Sin took occasion by the commandment and deceived me (vs. 8, 9). It is correct that when God touches down in revival, people get either glad or mad. The truth of God is either submitted to or rebelled against. When our natures are confronted and sin is revealed, there is a revival—a revival of sin. Like Custer, self takes a last stand.

Fact No. 4. The law slays us (vs. 11b). When self has had its last fling and we see ourselves for what we are, we are ready to die. All of us are like Die Hard batteries. We believe to the last, even though in a coma for days, that we will finally be able to live the Christian life through our efforts plus a little help from Christ. I remember as a pastor presenting these truths, and one day a lady said with fire flashing in her eyes, "I am sick and tired of you, and sick and tired of hearing you talk about Jesus all the time." The next day she came to the study to apologize and then she yielded to her death and began to experience Christ as her life. Self made a last stand as the law exposed her to the necessity of dying to self.

One evening after a crusade, a man who was then a pastor asked to talk about the service. With his wife, he had driven for several miles to be in the service. Margaret had already made the decision during the service to accept her death and claim Christ's life, but Jerry began objecting to the idea of dying. He said, "It's morbid to talk about dying. I almost have my doctorate in theology and I'm not going to buy something I've not thought through." They joined us for the prayer time in the host pastor's home, and when it came Jerry's time to pray he said, "Lord, I can't go on any longer. I'm ready to die and let you fill me with your Spirit and be my life." Instead of its being morbid Jerry's death made him one of the happiest men there. Today, Dr. Jerry Brock of Sedalia is one of America's outstanding evangelists.

Fact No. 5. The law shows up sin in its exceeding sinfulness (vs. 13). Standing before the law we see sin as God sees it. Isaiah cried out, *"Woe is me! for I am undone; because I am a man of unclean lips, and I dwell in the midst of a people of unclean lips; for mine eyes have seen the King, the Lord of hosts"* (Isaiah 6:5). His analysis in the previous chapter had been "Woe is them." He had repeated it again and again. Now he knew the truth and cried, *"Woe is me!"*

Fact No. 6. *The law is holy, just, and good*

(vs. 12). The law is just as holy and good as the great God who wrote it, and just as enduring. With a finger of fire, God wrote in rocks the ten principles by which each generation is to live before Him in righteousness. *"The law is spiritual"* (vs. 14), so the problem cannot be the law.

People who discover they have made church programs and church traditions to be their law should recognize that the problem is not with the law. I occasionally meet people who want to scrap all organization, planning, and methods. God never works in a vacuum or without order. The problem is not the systems we have turned into the law in our lives. Remember that Christ is the head of the body, not the hand. As the head of the body, He is to direct our plans, methods, and organization, not act as the hand to stamp His approval on what we've already made up our minds to do.

Fact No. 7. The facts are in; the law is not our problem. The process of elimination brings us to only one conclusion. Since our problem is not in the law, only one other possibility exists. The problem is within us. As Pogo, the comic strip character, said, "We have found the enemy . . . they is us." The problem of every Christian is the self life. As an unruly spiritual tyrant, the self refuses to be spiritual. Paul concluded, *"but I am carnal, sold under sin"* (vs. 14b). We are programmed to be sinful and never change.

No one more vividly points out the unchanging

nature in us than Miss Bertha Smith. Using her "anointed" flannelgraph, she shows how our nature is black and obstinate toward God. Characters from the Mandarin alphabet of the Chinese languages are placed on the board representing mankind. Each character is shaped much like the letter "A" in our alphabet. She then covers the black character with a red one, showing how the blood of Christ covers our sins. One character is chosen to represent her life. After reviewing forty years of mission service on the mainland of China and in Taiwan, and twenty years of service at home, she asks, "Has Miss Bertha changed by now after all these years? Let's see." She pulls back the red covering and the black character is right underneath, black as ever. Then she'll say, "Miss Bertha has not even paled; let's cover her up quickly." Sixty years of service, sixty years of prayer, and sixty years of taking the Word into her life and not changed! No, not even altered!

It's right at this point that most Christians are disillusioned. They assume they have changed through knowledge, experience, service, and honors bestowed. Like Isaiah, we hope the problem is with someone else ("Woe is them") but the problem always exists within us (*"Woe is me!"*). Someone has accurately pointed out that when we point our index finger at someone as the problem, the next three fingers are pressed against our palm pointing back at us. I am my problem, SOLD UNDER SIN. Only death can break the contract.

THE PROBLEM DESCRIBED (Face the Facts)

WHAT I DO, I UNDERSTAND NOT.

The good that I would, I do not.

WHAT I HATE, THAT I DO.

The unexplainable is happening in Paul. He concludes that the law is good, but he can't do what he admires so much. His self-centeredness is focused in three verses: 15, 16, and 17. One word "I" is repeated nine times. Paul suffers from "I" trouble. Thirty-eight times in the seventh chapter of Romans Paul refers to himself. He is consumed with self-consciousness.

When Christ-consciousness escapes us, our self-consciousness consumes us. A seesaw battle of self-admiration and self-condemnation rages. We defend and condemn ourselves all at the same time. A true story from a Tulsa newspaper illustrates the problem humorously:

JUDGE GETS VERDICT BY MAIL
Wichita, Kansas (AP)—The blizzard this week forced everyone to cope with unusual circumstances.

One Wichita man was scheduled to appear in Municipal Court Tuesday with a speeding charge. The court was closed because of the heavy snow, and the following letter arrived in the court clerk's office Friday:

"I was scheduled to be in court February 23,

1971, at 12:15 P.M. concerning a traffic ticket. Well, I was there as scheduled. And to my surprise I was the only one there. No one called and told me that court would be closed.

After going through the snow to be there on time, I decided to go ahead with the hearing as scheduled, which meant that I had to be the accuser (the patrolman who gave the citation) and I had to be the accused and also the judge.

The citation was for going 46 miles per hour in a 35 mile per hour zone. I had the speed alert on my car set on 44 miles per hour. As the accuser I felt that I was going over 35 miles per hour, but as the accused I knew that I was not going 46 miles per hour and as the judge, being the understanding man that I am, I decided to throw it out of court this time, but it had better not happen again."

THE PROBLEM DISCERNED
(Focus the Facts)

A new self told Paul to live up to the law; an old self, not crucified, defied the orders. So Paul discerned that *"it is no more I that do it, but sin that dwelleth in me"* (vs. 17). Then the moment of truth dawns: *"I know that in me (that is in my flesh) dwelleth no good thing"* (vs. 18a). The proud self wants to protest. "No good thing" seems an unfair exaggeration, yet the truth must stand. There is no good thing in us apart from Christ. Since EVERY GOOD THING IS IN CHRIST (Philemon 6), and Christ is in us, then we have every good thing within us, but the goodness is in His nature, not ours. The "ego busting" truth reduces us to our proper spiritual dimensions without Christ, which is zero. Darby once pointedly said, "When a man gets out of his own nothingness he gets into it."

Since no good thing is in the self life, "*how to perform that which is good I find not*" (vs. 18c) is the conclusion of every conscientious Christian. We have agreed with the oil company's motto, "It's performance that counts," but how can a "no gooder" be a "do gooder"? "How to perform" is a haunting question. Demands for performance have produced "Performing Arts Companies" among Christians, who perform with no right of reality in their productions.

During college days my initial major was speech, so I participated in several productions of College Theater at Southwest Missouri State College. Our instructor and director was a perfectionist. With certain techniques that she instilled in her students, Dr. Leslie Irene Coger demanded and often got near perfection. Lines were memorized early. Staging was structured carefully. Actions were rehearsed so each motion, even the batting of the eyelid, had meaning. In rehearsal she would stand in the middle of a nearly empty auditorium to listen. With line half said, or an action half executed, you'd be cut down with, "I don't believe you!" Lines, stage position, and actions may have been technically correct, but she demanded the intangible quality of realism. To be real we had to LOSE OUR IDENTITY. Instead of playing the character, we had to BE THE CHARACTER. It had to be more than a performance.

The world today shouts at many Christians who know the lines, are in the right place, and go through the right motions—"I don't believe you!" It's not performance that counts, but possession of His life; so it's not an act of imitating Christ, but a fact of His indwelling and being Himself. *"Because as he is so are we in this world"* (1 John 4:17b).

THE PROBLEM DISCONTINUED

"Consistency, thou art a jewel." Paul's consistency was his inconsistency. The "jewel" was his awareness things were getting NO BETTER. At the rate he was going, if he didn't slow down he'd back over something disastrous. The countdown to Paul's problems being discontinued can be clearly heard:

6 Dismay
   5 Disturbance
      4 Dissatisfaction
         3 Disgust
            2 Desperation

> 1 Death
>> 0 Decision to let Christ be his life.

We see Paul at the stage of desperation here. A war rages and there is no way to fight his war in peace. A final cry indicates honesty with himself: *"O wretched man that I am! who shall deliver me from the body of this death?"* (vs. 24). A wretched man admits it! A sentenced man agrees to it! The footsteps of the executioner can be heard in the corridor of his prison. If we did not know that victory soon will follow, the agony of this moment would be unbearable.

It was commonly known that near Tarsus, where Saul was born, a tribe of people used the most terrible means conceivable to execute a convicted murderer. The body of the victim was fastened to the body of the killer. After shoulder was tied to shoulder, back to back, thigh to thigh, arm to arm, they drove the murderer from the community. He was tied so tightly, he could not free himself; and after a few days, unable to eat, unable to sleep, death begot death. *"Who shall deliver me from the body of this death?"*

Admitting to himself that his case is hopeless, his condition terminal, he turns beyond himself and calls to another:

WHO SHALL DELIVER ME?
Not what, but who;

Not where, but who;
Not how, but who;
Not when, but who.

The executioner arrives. Instead of a ghoulish character from a dungeon, Paul sees the glorious character of Jesus Christ. *"I thank God through Jesus Christ, our Lord"* (vs. 25a).

THE PEACE OF EVERY CHRISTIAN

Romans 8:1–10

The word "therefore" marks the entry way into life in another dimension in Romans 8:1, just as in Romans 5:1. With a change in address from Sinai to Calvary, Paul finds no more condemnation. Bills from old sin accounts can't reach him at the new address. Threatening phone calls can no longer be dialed to the new phone number. *"There is therefore now no condemnation to them which are in Christ Jesus, who walk not after the flesh, but after the Spirit"* (8:1). *". . . to be spiritually minded in life and peace"* (8:6b).

PEACE THROUGH A COMPASSIONATE CHRIST

The Compassionate Conqueror

Paul lost his battle with the flesh, yet found himself winning the war. *"I see another law in my members warring against the law of my mind"* (7:23). The white flag of surrender was run up. *"Who shall deliver me?"* he asks, and the conqueror takes over. The conqueror is Christ! Now conquered by Christ, Paul is amazed that in his losing the battle, the war was won. The war was won for him by Christ to whom he surrendered. The victim is not the victor; the accused, the acquitted; the guilty, the innocent; the helpless, the strong.

Our Consciousness of Compassion

"*Now, no condemnation*" needs to cascade through the corridors of every Christian's heart. "*God sent not His son into the world to condemn the world; but that the world through him might be saved*" (John 3:17). Christ came to forgive, not to condemn. Many people have a regrettable image of Christ. They see Him in a referee's suit with whistle in mouth, flag in pocket, peering down so He can catch someone violating the rules and be able to blow the whistle, drop the penalty flag, and send him retreating at least fifteen yards spiritually.

If there is "no condemnation in Christ," why are so many Christians carrying such loads of guilt around with them today? Because they remove themselves from the benefits of Christ Himself. Every resident of Sinai feels condemned. A trip to Sinai will produce a "guilt trip" each time. It is appalling that so much done today by Christians is done out of guilt. Appeals are made for service on the basis of guilt—such as "Give, or God will be in bankruptcy by next week." We are never to give to God because He is in need. He has the cattle on a thousand hills. We are to give out of grace, not guilt, to get in on God's system of economy. "*And God is able to make all grace abound toward you: that ye, always having all sufficiency in all things, may abound to every good work*" (2 Corinthians 9:8). Giving out of grace lets us enjoy both the giving and the getting (Luke 6:38).

Christians in Galatia were set adrift on the sea of guilt:

> *I marvel that ye are so soon removed from him that called you into the Grace of Christ unto another gospel. . . . But now, after that ye have known God, or rather are known of God, how turn ye again to the weak and beggarly elements, whereunto ye desire again to be in bondage? . . . Stand fast therefore in the liberty wherewith Christ hath made us free, and be not entangled again with the yoke of bondage* (Galatians 1:6; 4:9; 5:1).

They had fallen from the good of Grace into the guilt of Gracelessness. I remember asking a study group once why Christians are chastened. A lady spoke up in an angry voice and said, "Because God's mad at us." I asked if that is what Scripture said. Again she stated her opinion. Recognizing that she would never give a scriptural answer, just an opinion, I quoted, ". . . *whom the Lord loveth he chasteneth*" (Hebrews 12:6a). Her problem is typical today. We don't see Christ as our refuge from condemnation.

Our guilt lies in expecting more of ourselves than God does. "*You are dead and your life is hid with Christ in God*" (Colossians 3:3) is His expectation of us. At one time in my life I was always setting goals instead of "grace markers." If you set a goal you must attain it. If you set a "grace marker," you expect God's supply of power in Christ to enable you to achieve (Philippians 3:14). Goal-setting is a characteristic of successful people, so I wanted to join their fraternity. (Incidentally, I don't expect less than success now in Christ.) Like Benjamin Franklin, who scrapped his system, I became quite discouraged. My goals were either too high or I was too short. I'd say to the Lord after not reaching the goal of enough study time, "I've let you down." Or when a sermon designed for the annual "Best Sermon of the Year Award" crashed without even leaving the runway, I'd repeat, "Lord, I've let you down." One day the Lord said to me intuitively, "Jim, you didn't let me down, because you weren't even holding me up." That's an "ego buster," to be sure, but it's also a "guilt evaporator."

PEACE THROUGH THE CONTROLLING OF THE FLESH

The conditions for God's peace to be unabating are clearly set out. We are to "*walk not after the flesh, but after the Spirit*" (8:4). We are admonished in Galatians 5:16 to *"Walk in the Spirit, and ye shall not fulfil the lust of the flesh."*

The flesh is simply the human personality apart from God's control. It is man on his own. As a trichotomy of spirit, soul, and body, we were designed for Spirit mastery. Without Christ we are inverted so that body and soul dominate a spirit not even inhabited by the Holy Spirit. As Christians, we are indwelt by the Holy Spirit (Romans 8:9b). While we may have the benefits of His residency, we may not be experiencing the power of His presidency. Thus a Christian may walk in the flesh which is under death sentence, instead of walking in the Spirit which is under Life's Sovereign. The control of the Spirit in us controls the nature of the flesh. So the Scripture says to walk in Spirit control and the Spirit will negate the flesh. Too often people invert that truth in their attempt to be free from the contemptible flesh or old self-life. They resolve, "I'll not walk in the flesh; then I can walk in the Spirit. I refuse to be upset with my neighbor whose dog chases my cat, so today I'll not think about them, so I can walk in the Spirit. Why anyone would even keep a mongrel like that, I don't for the life of me know. So, I'll not think about them, but that dog barks louder at night. . . ." The attempt at NOT thinking has spawned a runaway thinker. It's like the story of B'rer Rabbit and the Tar Baby. The harder B'rer Rabbit struggled to get rid of the Tar Baby, the more "stuck up" he became.

The harder we try to get rid of proud flesh, the more "stuck up" we become.

Our flesh is like a Pandora's Box. To live out of the resources of the flesh, we must open it and anything conceivable can fly out. *"Now the doings (practices) of the flesh are clear—obvious: they are immorality, impurity, indecency; idolatry, sorcery, enmity, strife, jealousy, anger (ill temper), selfishness, divisions (dissensions), party spirit (factions, sects with peculiar opinions, heresies); Envy, drunkenness, carousing, and the like"* (Galatians 5:19-21a Amplified Bible). As inclusive as this list of practices is, it is open ended. "And the like" means that our nature may emit any other conceivable thing.

I once saw a vivid illustration used in a sermon by Dr. John B. Wright, pastor of the First Baptist Church of Little Rock, Arkansas. Holding a full glass of water in his hand, he told the congregation, "Whatever we are full of is what spills out when we are bumped." My closest friend from earliest days of preaching struck the glass and water spilled out all over the new carpet in the new sanctuary. "The glass was full of water, so when I bumped it, water spilled out," he emphasized. Then in a sermon titled "A False Filling" he acknowledged some spillage from his own life that was not from the Lord. A hushed congregation that filled the building came to love him all the more for his transparency. They saw in the spillage of some attitudes he acknowledged that our "bumps" in life reveal who's really controlling us. God allows us to be bumped so all that is unacceptable in our nature can be exposed. Then we can be filled with the fruit of the Spirit.

PEACE THROUGH A CONCEPT OF THE CARNAL MIND

The *Power of Positive Thinking* as verbalized by Dr. Norman Vincent Peale is so intriguing, thousands have exercised their minds in the spas of positive calisthenics. Who doesn't want to think his or her way to satisfaction? But "if Paul is appealing, Peale is appalling," to quote Dr. Vance Havner. The converse would also be true. If Peale is appealing, Paul is appalling, for they are diametrically opposed in their positions. Peale advocates "the power of positive thinking." Paul advocates the "power of the Positive Thinker." Without the power of the Positive Thinker, we can't think positively. Paul says our minds are enemies of the positive and friends of the negative.

For those who are according to the flesh and controlled by its unholy desires, set their minds on and pursue those things which gratify the flesh. But those who are according to the Spirit and [controlled by the desires] of the Spirit, set their minds on and seek those things which gratify the (Holy) Spirit. Now the mind of the flesh [which is sense and reason without the Holy Spirit] is death—death that comprises all the miseries arising from sin, both here and hereafter. But the mind of the (Holy) Spirit is life and soul-peace [both now and forever]. [That is] because the mind of the flesh—with its carnal thoughts and purposes—is hostile to God; for it does not submit itself to God's Law, indeed it cannot (Romans 8:5-7 Amplified Bible).

Without a proper concept of the carnal mind, many of us have labored under the illusion that we are friends of God, while in spiritual reality we are at enmity against God. It also relieves us to know at last the reason for mental backlashes that leave our spiritual continuity so snarled.

After becoming a Christian at age sixteen and wanting to be a one hundred percenter, I was mortified at thoughts that whizzed in my mind like "bats in my belfry." At times when I tried to pray, horrendous thoughts cropped up and my desire to pray crumbled before their attack. With nets, noise makers, and other bat exterminators, I'd go up in the "belfry" of my mind and try to clean out the thoughts that so embarrassed and exasperated me. A part of my agony was in assuming I was the only Christian who had that same conflict. Christians I was around played the game of "let's pretend" so convincingly, I never dreamed many of them also hurt and "wore bandages" deep within.

During the fourteen years of this conflict, I was

pastor of a church. When I was a senior in high school, I started pastoring a church that was dying and had nothing to lose. During those years, I concluded that, as Hannah Whitall Smith says, the only way to get rid of my headache would be to get rid of my head. So I resolved to endure the one because I must keep the other.

Then God planted in the path of my life a "salty" Christian. As the salt of the earth, a "salty" Christian makes you thirsty if you're spiritually dry, and irritates you if you have spiritual hurts. Dr. James H. Smith, now Executive Secretary of Illinois Baptists, did both. He made me thirsty for the relaxed, free approach to life that I saw in him, and he irritated me because I had hurts. At an assembly where I served as president, he became more transparent than anyone I'd ever heard. When I discovered he'd had "bats in his belfry" too, inwardly I whistled a sigh of relief and thought "I'm not the only one." Then he went on to tell of the victory he'd found in Christ. Irritation followed, for I was still stuck with the "bats in my belfry."

How did I get rid of the "bats"? I didn't! A few months after that conference with Dr. Smith, I made an unconditional surrender to Christ. The bats got locked up. I don't go up there now with nets, noisemakers, and bat exterminators. I'm having so much enjoyment in a new dimension of my life that I simply don't go back to the belfry anymore. When a "bat" does get loose occasionally, I concentrate on Christ. His mind in me puts my bats under lock and key.

Since I have presented this principle openly in seven years of travel, many little white-haired ladies who are only one step from glorification have whispered, "You know, I have that problem with my thoughts too." The carnal mind will always be an enemy at any age, at any level of dedication, at any place of service. It is an enemy of faith, it is an enemy of prayer, it is an enemy of witnessing, it is an enemy of Bible study; for it is an enemy of God.

The power of the Positive Thinker "*shall keep your hearts and minds through Christ Jesus*" (Philippians 4:7b). "*For God hath not given us the spirit of fear, but of power, and of love, and a sound mind*" (2 Timothy 1:7), as you "*let this mind be in you, which was also in Christ Jesus*" (Philippians 2:5).

PEACE THOUGH THERE IS THE CLASHING OF ARMS

The War Continues; We Don't

When the "life and peace" of the spiritual mind mentioned in verse 6 is operative, that peace does not mean an absence of war, as many have concluded. The war is not terminated . . . the old self-life is, thus granting peace. Through the termination of the self-life and the realization of the

Christ-life, the war is relocated. We are not positioned in Christ in the euphoria of an isolation chamber. Instead, we are placed right in the middle of the battle itself. The battle front once so loud from within is all quiet. The front is now all around us. Yet the outer clashing of arms need not disturb the tranquility of the inner peace.

The very rules of semantics dictate that if you know victory you must know war. If you know peace, you have at one time or another known war. In Revelation we read an account of the spiritual battle that has raged from the time

> . . . *war broke out in heaven, Michael and his angels going forth to battle with the dragon; and the dragon and his angels fought, But they were defeated and there was no room found for them in heaven any longer. And the huge dragon was cast down and out, that ages-old serpent, who is called the Devil and Satan, he who is the seducer (deceiver) of all humanity the world over; he was forced out and down to the earth, and his angels were flung out along with him* (Revelation 12:7-9 Amplified Bible).

An armistice to this, the longest and fiercest of all wars, will be realized only when Christ returns to earth.

Peace in the Presence of Your Enemies

The principle of inner peace in the midst of outer war can be seen throughout Scripture. *"Thou preparest a table before me in the presence of mine enemies"* (Psalm 23:5). That's a curious place to prepare a table, don't you think? Yet there it is, right in the presence of your enemies.

A few summers ago my family was with me while I conducted a crusade in Loveland, Colorado, gateway to Estes Park. One day we packed a picnic lunch and drove toward the park between yawning walls of rock in Big Thompson Canyon. At a beautiful spot alongside a rushing mountain stream, we spread our lunch on the picnic table. No sooner had we uncovered the food than squadrons of yellow jacket bees began practicing their landing and take-offs. We had a table before us in the presence of our enemies. I said, "We'll have to move or get stung." So we loaded up everything, got back in the Suburban, and drove two or three miles farther up. The scene was exactly the same; water rushed hurriedly over rock in the stream, rock walls towered with beauty and awesome strength above, and—the same yellow jackets continued their flight training. Concluding that another move would probably only bring a repeat performance, we started eating from the table set before us. Then I discovered that if I would concentrate on the table and not on the enemies, they circled harmlessly around. So we enjoyed the table set before us in the presence of our enemies.

Don't Fight; Sing

Through the centuries, people have experienced cold war, hot war, civil war, limited war, nuclear war, and world war, but only God can let you experience PEACEFUL WAR. Another scriptural account of this peaceful war can be seen in 2 Chronicles 20:10-25.

THERE WAS A BATTLE TO FIGHT. Jehoshaphat, king of the southern kingdom of Judah, went to pray. Like the lady who after reading the morning paper prayed, "Lord, if you read the paper this morning you know we're in a mess," he told the Lord that they were surrounded and outnumbered by a triumvirate of three powers—Ammon, Moab, and Mount Seir. In verse 12, he prayed three things that all real prayer involves: (1) "we have no might" (admitting our nothingness); (2) "we don't know what to do" (admitting our lack of knowledge); and (3) "our eyes are on you" (turning beyond ourselves to Christ).

THERE WAS A VICTORY TO CLAIM. The Lord said to a beleagured nation, *"Be not afraid or dismayed by reason of this great multitude; for the battle is not yours, but God's"* (vs. 15). *"Ye shall not need to fight in this battle . . . stand ye still, and see the salvation of the Lord with you"* (vs.

17). So instead of fighting a battle already lost, they were to claim a victory already won.

THERE WAS A SONG TO SING. The most amazing military science and tactics ever witnessed then followed. The Lord enrolled the army in a choir and gave them a chorus to sing, *"Praise the Lord; for his mercy endureth forever"* (vs. 21).

They went out singing in peace.

God went out fighting in power.

THERE WERE SPOILS TO GATHER. The armies of Ammon, Moab, and Mount Seir were annihilated as they destroyed one another. The people of God spent three enjoyable and very profitable days *"gathering of the spoil, it was so much"* (vs. 25b). We can spend the rest of our lives gathering the spoil of Christ's victories as we fight A PEACEFUL WAR.

PEACE THROUGH THE COMPLETENESS OF CHRIST'S ARMOR

From within and without, Christ is our armor in the battle. We are indwelt by Christ: *"But you are not in the flesh, but in the Spirit, if so be that the Spirit of God dwell in you. Now if any man have not the Spirit of Christ, he is none of his. And if Christ be in you, the body is dead because of sin, but the Spirit is life because of righteousness"* (Romans 8:9-10). We are also privileged to *"put (ye) on the Lord Jesus Christ and make not provision for the flesh, to fulfil the lust thereof"* (Romans 13:14). To put on the WHOLE ARMOR

OF GOD as Ephesians 6:11 instructs, we put on, through the appropriation of faith, Jesus Christ, who is our armor. With Christ our armor about us, and Christ our life within us, we are armed within and without.

The brevity of this book does not permit me to deal in detail with principles of "spiritual warfare," but I will do this in a second book, a study of Ephesians, which is a sequel to Romans in spiritual progression.

THE POWER OF EVERY CHRISTIAN

Romans 8:11–39

An interesting encounter with electrical power awaited me in Australia in 1969. The first morning in the city of Sydney, I plugged in my electric razor and it took off with an enthusiasm I had never known it to have. It hummed with such determination, I wondered if it was in training to replace a jet motor on a Boeing 707. After shaving, I commented to my host pastor that my razor had lots of get up and go in his country. He looked shocked and concerned as he said, "Oh, no! I was supposed to give you a transformer to break the power down from 220 to 110." I had plugged into a greater power source than usual as I plugged into 220. The razor had not burned up, but did it ever speed up!

Too often we plod along on 110, but our spiritual power is limitless. A greater POWER SOURCE is available to all of us as Christians.

THE PROMISE OF POWER: *"But ye shall receive power, after that the Holy Spirit is come upon you; and ye shall be witnesses unto me"* (Acts 1:8a).

THE POSSESSION OF POWER: *"But if the Spirit of him that raised up Jesus from the dead dwell in you, he that raised up Christ from the dead shall also* [give life to] *your mortal bodies by his Spirit that dwelleth in you"* (Romans 8:11).

THE PARTAKING OF POWER: *"That I may know him, and the power of his resurrection, and the fellowship of his sufferings, being made conformable unto his death"* (Philippians 3:10).

THE PROMISE OF POWER was fulfilled!!

THE POSSESSION OF POWER is yours by *"his Spirit that dwelleth in you"* (vs. 11b). The same Holy Spirit who emptied a tomb 1900 years ago with the most awesome demonstration of power ever witnessed is in you right now!

THE PARTAKING OF POWER is your privilege daily.

THE PROSPECT OF POWER for you will excite you as nothing else can, unless, of course, your "exciter" is turned completely off.

CHRIST AND HIS POWER SOURCE

It's been only in the second half of my Christian life, which has been the most exciting half, that I have been aware of Christ's power source for living. As the second person of the trinity, Christ lived His life in the power of the Holy Spirit, the third person of the trinity. In fact, Christ's entire life from birth through resurrection was achieved by the power of the Holy Spirit.

Holy Spirit Power for Birth

The first birth announcement of Jesus Christ was given Mary by an angel: *"Fear not Mary, for thou hast found favour with God. And, behold, thou shalt conceive in thy womb and bring forth a son, and shalt call his name Jesus.... The Holy Ghost shall come upon thee, and the power of the Highest shall overshadow thee: therefore also that holy thing which shall be born of thee shall be called the Son of God"* (Luke 1:30, 31, & 35). Thus the earthly life of Christ could begin because of a spiritual conception and a spiritual birth. Christ was the only person in history who was as old as his Father and older than his mother.

Holy Spirit Power for Life

Just as His earthly life began in the power of the Spirit, it continued in the power of the Spirit.

IN TEMPTATION: *"And Jesus being full of the Holy [Spirit] returned from Jordan, and was led by the Spirit into the wilderness"* (Luke 4:1).

IN MINISTRY: *"And Jesus returned in the power of the Spirit into Galilee: and there went out a fame of him through all the region around about"* (Luke 4:14).

IN SERVICE: *"The Son can do nothing of Himself"* (John 5:19).

IN SPEAKING: *". . . the words that I speak unto*

you, they are spirit, and they are life" (John 6:63b).

Holy Spirit Power for Death

Even in death Jesus drew from the grace of God's provision of power. Without fear and with perfect love ruling, he forgave a thief and refused to strike back at those who had struck Him. *"But we see Jesus, who was made a little lower than the angels for the suffering of death, crowned with glory and honour; that he by the grace of God should taste death for every man"* (Hebrews 2:9).

Holy Spirit Power for Resurrection

"But if the Spirit of him that raised up Jesus from the dead dwell in you, he that raised up Christ from the dead shall also [give life to] your mortal bodies by his Spirit that dwelleth in you" (Romans 8:11).

His return from the vale of death was achieved by the Holy Spirit.

THREE TERMS—ONE LIFE

Because the Holy Spirit was Christ's life, Paul interchangeably used three sets of terms:

1. The Spirit filled life;
2. The Christ-life;
3. The life of faith.

All three terms are found in Ephesians 3:16-17a: *"That he would grant you, according to the riches of his glory, to be strengthened with might by his Spirit in the inner man; That Christ may dwell in your hearts by faith."* The one normal New Testament Christian life can be verbalized with all three sets of terms. It is unfortunate indeed that many are lost today on the "semantic desert," bickering over terms.

THE INWARD POWER SOURCE

As we have just seen, the Holy Spirit produced Christ's conception into His earthly life 1900 years ago. He is within you right now to reproduce Christ's life through you in the twentieth century. Many people have been conditioned to fear the Holy Spirit, lest He lead them off on a tangent of radicalism. I am not afraid of Pentecost or of the Holy Spirit, however, for on that day He made Christ so real that three thousand people wanted Him. The Holy Spirit is the only power source by which Christ can be seen through me.

A few years ago I toured an atomic reactor on California's coast. My host was an employee of the company operating the reactor. He informed me of the enormous amount of electrical power being generated from that one atomic reactor. That energy was lighting the coastal region, turning great motors in industry, opening doors for hurried shoppers, causing stereos to play beautiful music for tired people wanting rest, and doing a myriad of other things. As I stood there looking at that concentration of power, I smiled as I realized that in my body right then, taking up only a fraction of the space of that reactor, was more power than all the atomic reactors in the world combined. In me was the One who turned Jesus loose from death, hell, and the grave.

It is inconceivable that such a power potential for beginning each day, living each day, and ending each day, could be overlooked. Yet so many never seem to draw from this POWER SOURCE. I have never forgotten stepping from a pastor's car on the church parking lot as we arrived for Sunday School and greeting a lady just leaving her car. I said, "Good morning! It's a wonderful day, isn't it?" She groaned, "No, it's not; as a matter of fact it's terrible." She hastened to explain, "I told the nominating committee I couldn't teach that class and I've spent the night unable to sleep for fear of facing them." In her hand she carried a volume containing sixty-six books. In her heart she carried the Author of all sixty-six books. Yet, not being aware of the potential residing in her, she walked to that class in fear and defeat.

As a Christian, you are a walking power plant! A spiritual reactor is within! Start life's operations now out of this POWER SOURCE.

THE OUTWARD POWER SOURCE

Letting Christ out is just as exciting as letting Christ in. The average Christian has heard repeatedly how to let Christ in, but so little about how to let Him out. Another "therefore" opens the door to the lab again in verse 12.

A Quick Refresher in Review

"Therefore, brethren, we are debtors, not to the flesh, to live after the flesh. For if ye live after the flesh, ye shall die: but if ye through the Spirit do mortify the deeds of the body, ye shall live" (vs. 12-13).

Paul gives a quick review. *"Owe no man any thing"* (Romans 13:8), particularly the old self. You're not a debtor to the flesh, so don't plunge back into introspection and start to pay off anything you may think you have owed to yourself. Through the power of the Spirit, put to death the evil deeds the body suggests and really enjoy living now.

Be Led—Be Like the Family

"For as many as are led by the Spirit of God, they are the sons of God" (vs. 14).

"Being led by the Spirit" means we move in cadence with Christ's count. Do "being led" and "being sons of God" mean that only the people being led are Christians? No! For we have already seen it is possible to be a Christian, yet not walk in the Spirit. "Being sons of God" means we bear a family resemblance. We walk like, talk like, think like, pray like, believe like, give like, witness like—a child of God.

Be Free—Be Worshipping

"For ye have not received the spirit of bondage again to fear; but ye have received the Spirit of adoption, whereby we cry, Abba, Father" (vs. 15). Lazarus was a welcome sight when he emerged from that tomb on the most eventful day in Bethany. But an appearance by Lazarus as he was before he was LOOSED AND LET GO, would have been repulsive rather than attractive. He was loosed from the grave clothes to be FREE INDEED. We have not received bondage again, but freedom in Him. Why climb back into graveclothes you've already taken off? God has given you a conquering faith.

Instead of the bondage of fear, you have the blessing of adoration from within. The Spirit of adoption enables us to adore our Lord as the Spirit cries from within, "ABBA, FATHER." Jesus said, *". . . true worshippers shall worship the Father in Spirit and in truth: for the Father seeketh such to worship him"* (John 4:23). Until the Spirit controls us, we can't really worship, nor can we worship truthfully. With the Spirit controlling, we can't keep from worshipping, nor can we keep from worshipping truthfully.

Thousands today worship worship. How many worship the Lord? In Hosea's day, altars were on every hilltop, but people didn't worship God. Today, churches are on many street corners in America. Yet many punch the time clock at 10:45 on Sunday morning, holding their pulse to be sure they will make it, watching their watch to be sure the preacher will finish—on time—and call it worship.

The Spirit's cry of "ABBA, FATHER" doesn't start at 11:00 or end at 12:00 on Sunday morning. Instead He cries in adoration from within, so that *"whatsoever you do in word or deed, do all in the name of the Lord Jesus, giving thanks to God and the Father by him"* (Colossians 3:17). Sunday morning worship services that are a continuation of a service on Friday afternoon at work, or a Saturday afternoon on the golf course, or a prayer meeting Saturday night, are always great services.

Be Aware—Be a Child of the King

"The Spirit (Himself) beareth witness with our spirit, that we are the children of God" (vs. 16).

As the Holy Spirit is enthroned in our lives, He takes the witness stand. He raises His right hand and pledges to tell the truth, the whole truth, and nothing but the truth. (As He is God, He won't need help.) He starts telling the truth that you are saved! Your spirit knows peace with God. He goes on telling you the whole truth . . . don't stop until you learn all he will testify to.

It's easy to forget whose child you are. Sometimes the accuser (Satan) accuses you; sometimes your actions accuse you; sometimes people accuse you. Let the Holy Spirit take the stand and testify that you are a child of God. As you listen, you will become aware of all you became when you became His child. A pastor friend, Gene Casey, always closes his telephone calls to his children away from home with an admonition, "Now don't forget whose child you are." It's easy to forget you are a child of the King.

A few years ago I was in San Antonio during the same time that Miss Corrie ten Boom was ministering there. I rode with Jack Taylor when he took Miss Corrie and her associate, Ellen Kraum, to the airport for departure. On the way back, Jack said he had asked Miss Corrie during the week if she thought his new car was too expensive for a preacher to be driving. She had thought a moment and said, "Ah, no, it is not too much for a child of the King" from one who knows so well that "it's not too much for a child of the King" to suffer persecution—that is even more remarkable! "It's not too much for a child of the King" to be abased or exalted! Paul knew that, come what may, "It's not too much for a child of the King!"

Be a Joint Heir—Be as He Is

"And if children, then heirs; heirs of God, and joint heirs with Christ; if so be that we suffer with

him, that we may be also glorified together" (vs. 17). As a child of the King we have become a joint heir. There is a distinct difference between being an heir and a joint heir. A joint partner owns the whole and their half, an attorney friend has affirmed to me. While the joint partners live, they each own the whole and the half that is theirs. If one of them dies, the other owns all. But if three children are heirs to an estate, the estate is divided into three equal parts between them. If they are joint heirs, however, they can each say, "I have all the estate," for any part of it is theirs.

As a joint heir with Christ:

All He did we share in.
All He is we are.
All He has we have.
All He does we obtain.
All He will do we benefit from.

Listen to His prayer for us as joint heirs:

I pray for them: I pray not for the world, but for them which thou hast given me; for they are thine. And all mine are thine, and thine are mine; and I am glorified in them. . . . Father, keep through thine own name those whom thou hast given me, that they may be one, as we are . . . that they might have my joy fulfilled in themselves. . . . Neither pray I for these alone, but for them also which shall believe on me

through their word; That they all may be one,
as thou, Father, art in me, and I in thee, that
they also may be one in us (John 17:9-11, 13,
20, 21a).

To be as He is means we shall share in His suffering
and in His Glory. Just as the POWER OF HIS RESUR-
RECTION is real, so the FELLOWSHIP OF HIS SUF-
FERINGS is as real.

"I reckon that the sufferings of this present time
are not worthy to be compared with the glory
which shall be revealed in us" (vs. 18).

Some Ways He Suffers — Some Ways We Suffer

1. The Suffering of the Body of Christ

In a physical body an arm injury may send the
whole body to bed in shock. Pain in a tooth may
produce a severe headache, known medically as
referred pain. When a brother or sister suffers, the
head of the Church suffers, and as fellow members
of the body in fellowship with the head, we suffer.
Christ asked Saul, "Why do you persecute me?"
Every blow that Saul has directed against a Christian had fallen on Christ vicariously. We vicariously share also in that referred pain.

2. We Suffer the Anguish of Sins Committed

Christ had no anguish over His own sins, for He
had none; yet the suffering He bore for our sins
cannot be fathomed by our finite minds. As Chris-

tians we suffer the inner agony of realizing that old-self has taken the throne of our lives again, leaving muddy footprints on white carpet while getting there. Sin in the life of a Spiritually sensitized Christian brings inner suffering.

3. We Suffer in Vicarious Intercession

Even as Jesus suffered in intercession, so may we. *"Who in the days of His flesh, when he had offered up prayers and supplications with strong crying and tears unto him that was able to save him from death.... Though he were a Son, yet learned he obedience by the things which he suffered"* (Hebrews 5:7, 8). With great anguish we are taken at times in prayer into the vicarious agony of those for whom we pray. John Hyde, known as Praying Hyde, prayed out his life in India, seeing thousands come to Christ. His body broke under the agony of the spiritual battle he was fighting.

4. The Suffering of a Burden For a Lost World

The world that Jesus loved hated Him in return. He wept for a city that would in a matter of hours gleefully put Him to death. Don't be astonished if your total identification with Christ spawns reaction of the same kind.

These things have I spoken unto you that ye should not be offended. They shall put you out of the synagogues; yea, the time cometh that whosoever killeth you will think that he doeth

God service. And these things will they do unto you, because they have not known the Father, nor me. . . . In the world you shall have tribulation: but be of good cheer; I have overcome the world (John 16:1-3, 33).

5. We Suffer the Calamity That Befalls All

IT RAINS ON THE JUST AND THE UNJUST, so calamity comes to Christians and lost alike. Christians have fellowship as they walk in the sufferings of calamity, whereas the lost walk alone.

BUT OH THE GLORY!!! ". . . *the sufferings of this present time are not worthy to be compared with the glory which shall be revealed in us*" (Romans 8:18).

Don't erroneously conclude that the space on suffering in this book is an ominous threat to your future. I have included it because some have naively believed that with Christ in control, they will have no more problems. With Christ in control we may have more problems than ever, but we have a problem-solver lost people don't have, and the sufferings can't even compare to the glory.

Dr. C. L. Culpepper told me that in China the Chinese pastors who were beaten and tortured by the Communists until unconscious told him with a glow of joy on their faces that even in the agony of physical pain, God sent waves of inner power through them to comfort them. A medical doctor said to me one night after a study session in Romans, "I know now how the early Christians went singing to the stake to be burned or to the Roman circus arenas to have the lions turned on them." He continued, "How they did it always bothered me, for I knew I lacked that kind of courage." None of us knows what we may suffer—some of my closest friends have borne great hurts this past year. But we do know what we shall receive: GLORY SHALL BE REVEALED IN US.

THE UPWARD POWER SOURCE

A Yearning Universe

For the earnest expectation of the [creation] waiteth for the manifestation of the sons of God. For the [creation] was made subject to vanity, not willingly, but by reason of him who hath subjected the same in hope. Because the [creation] itself also shall be delivered from the bondage of corruption into the glorious liberty of the children of God. For we know that the whole creation groaneth and travaileth in pain together until now (Romans 8:19-22).

All of the universe is yearning for reinstatement in the original order of creation. With ecological imbalances flashing warning signals throughout God's natural system, it is apparent that man is a poor gardener in the earthly garden of God's creation. There is good evidence that a global greenhouse was once in operation all over this earth. "*And God said, Let there be a firmament in the midst of the waters, and let it divide the waters from the waters. And God made the firmament, and divided the waters which were under the firmament from the waters which were above the firmament: and it was so*" (Genesis 1:6-7). Today, creation yearns to get back under the canopy of God's initial creation.

This tired and tottering universe of ours is also simply groaning with the pain of growing old. In his book *The Bible and Science*, Dr. Henry M. Morris writes, "The second law of thermodynamics states that in any real process or system in which energy is being transformed into other forms, at least some of it is transformed into heat energy which cannot be converted back into other useful forms . . . this law expresses the fact that in any closed system there must always be a decrease of order or organization." Like an aged person who groans getting out of the rocker, or sighs when lying down for a nap, our universe is wearily waiting for the creator to come as King and remake it. This time there will be a new heaven and a new earth combined. Then the yearning world can say: "*For, lo, the winter is past, the rain is over and gone; The flowers appear on the earth; the time of the singing of birds is come*" (The Song of Solomon 2:11, 12).

A Yearning Redeemed Body

"*And not only they, but ourselves also, which have the first-fruits of the Spirit, even we ourselves groan within ourselves, waiting for the adoption, to wit, the redemption of our body*" (vs. 23).

The universe with its groanings or yearnings to be restored to "the good 'young' days" is not alone. Our bodies also have a yearning for restoration to the "good life." Even the body responds to the urge of the Holy Spirit to end the enmity between the spirit and the flesh that the body may be clothed again with the glory of God as Adam and Eve were. Since the human personality is the highest order of God's creation, man is even more eager to return to the position when God made the assessment "very good."

In that coming resurrected body, we will appear in the image of the second Adam, Jesus Christ, even as now we are in the image of the first Adam. "... *we know that, when he shall appear, we shall be like him; for we shall see him as he is*" (1 John 3:2).

"*For our [citizenship] is in heaven; from whence also we look for the Savior, the Lord Jesus Christ: Who shall change [the body of our humiliation], that it may be fashioned like unto his [glorified] body, according to the working where-*

by he is able even to subdue all things unto himself"
(Philippians 3:20, 21).

The cry of David is the cry of all the redeemed,
"*I shall be satisfied, when I awake, with thy
likeness*" (Psalm 17:15).

THE PRAYER POTENTIAL OF EVERY CHRISTIAN

Romans 8:26–27

All Christians suffer a common infirmity, a limitation: we do not know how to pray, nor what to pray for. Not knowing God's "game plan," we don't know what plays to call when huddled for prayer. *"We know not what we should pray for as we ought"* (vs. 26b). We know we "ought" to pray, yet we can't pray as we "ought." Dwelling within us, as a prayer partner in residence, is the Holy Spirit, the most proficient person in prayer that ever prayed. He is anxiously waiting to enroll us in a course of productive prayer.

An illustration of frustrated praying was demonstrated to me in Taiwan in 1970. Because of the hurried schedule we kept in the crusades, missionaries took us to officers' clubs at the U.S. Military installations on the island. While eating lunch one day, I needed to cash a traveler's check. I was directed to the money exchange cashier in the game room, which consisted mainly of gambling devices. Around the room military personnel were playing the machines. I was intrigued by their actions. Some used systems, some used none, but all looked bored, as with glassy stares at nothing they poked in a coin and pulled the handle, poked in a coin and pulled the handle. I'd seen something quite similar somewhere . . . it suddenly dawned on me . . . PRAYER MEETING ON WEDNES-DAY NIGHT! With monotonous repetition I'd heard people poke in the prayer and pull the handle, poke in the prayer and pull the handle. Both in the prayer meeting and there in that gambling room the object was to get a lucky hit. I've heard people pray for the sick and plan the funeral all at the same time. The Christians who prayed for Peter's release from prison kept him at the gate, unable to get in, after an angel of God had freed him from prison. When Peter continued knocking persistently, they finally went to the gate and "were astonished." They weren't expecting him! (Acts 12:5-17). That's like praying for rain, then not carrying an umbrella. All of us can truthfully say, "Teacher, teach us to pray." "*We know not what we should pray for as we ought*" (vs. 26).

The Holy Spirit Yearns to Make Praying Practical

Scripture declares that all requests made under the Holy Spirit's direction are answered for "*He maketh intercession for the saints according to the will of God*" (vs. 27). Praying in the Spirit is not a "lucky hit" but a carefully directed spiritual procedure.

Let me illustrate with a recent experience how we can be directed by the Holy Spirit in our praying. Two men flew me home from Norman, Oklahoma, recently in what I shall choose to call their "Twin Bill Airlines." Neither Bill Duncan nor Bill Higginbotham had ever been to West Plains, Missouri, before. "They knew not what to aim for as they ought." As soon as we were airborne, the latest radio equipment on their new twin Cessna came into play. With the two-way communication system keeping us informed of locations, we spanned the distance at over 200 miles an hour. (What a way to come home!) The perfect landing was no accident but was a carefully directed procedure, just as prayer must be. Now look at the procedure:

1. A Willingness To be Involved: A desire to get me home in the shortest amount of time, so I could devote that entire week to writing, made the men willing to become involved. Likewise, we cannot pray without a release of our wills to the Holy Spirit. *"He works in us both to will and to do according to His good pleasure"* (Philippians 2:13). To be directable in prayer, we must be willing. If we're not, then we should simply pray, "Lord, I am not willing, but I am willing to be made willing."

2. A Willingness to Follow Signals: While we were in the air the omni signals were obeyed. Praying in the Spirit means we listen as much as we talk, if not more so. Early in my pilgrimage in

directed prayer, I was given Glen Clark's book *I Will Lift Up Mine Eyes*. He relates how as a boy growing up in New England before the days of vacuum sweepers, they swept rugs by taking them outside and hanging them on the clothesline. In winter they would throw snow into the rug. By sweeping the snow off they could see that all the rug was covered in their sweeping. The dust they could not see, but when the snow was gone they knew the rug was clean. In praying, he said he learned to saturate his mind with what he was to pray about (throw the snow in the rug) then hold it up before the Lord. If peace came (the snow was swept off), then he could believe the Lord for the answer to that prayer, for it was the will of God. If the peace of God did not come, then he did not proceed on that point until peace came. Miss Bertha Smith tells of starting to pray for Mrs. Culpepper in China when the Holy Spirit checked her. She was reminded of resentment she had toward another missionary. That had to be dealt with before she could pray on to victory for Mrs. Culpepper. It is necessary to follow the Holy Spirit's signals.

3. A Willingness to Fly the Map: With the flight chart laid out before them at all times, the pilots kept a running check on our location. God has also given us a map for our prayer life. When with an open Bible we pray according to the Word of God, we are assured we are praying the

will of God. We can "watch and pray"—watch the Bible and pray.

4. A Willingness to Land on Target: It is very easy to overshoot or undershoot a runway. When we follow the Holy Spirit's instructions, we must learn to come right to the PLACE, the PERSON, and the PLAN in prayer that the Holy Spirit is leading us to. Paul asked three times for the thorn's removal from his flesh. Each time he learned that his destination didn't stop with the thorn, but was to go on to the claiming of the "Grace sufficient for thee." So instead of being directed to a "thorn removed," he was directed to a "Grace received" (2 Corinthians 12:2-9).

Now this short course on prayer is not sufficient for flights under all weather conditions. I recommend you take further studies under Andrew Murray in *With Christ in the School of Prayer*.

The Holy Spirit Yearns to Make Praying Powerful

The enormous power potential we have already seen is waiting to be moved out of storage and into action by the Holy Spirit. One of the awesome aspects of praying in the Spirit, as you are directed to the purpose God has in mind, is to realize He will do even more than you ever imagined. "*Now unto Him that is able to do exceeding abundantly above all that we ask or think, according to the power that worketh in us*" (Ephesians 3:20). Just as the cripple sat at the gate called beautiful and begged for "alms" and got "legs," so we receive all the power of Christ's victory as we pray in the Spirit.

A banking experience several years ago became a lesson on prayer for me. Accompanied by my friend John Wright, I went to a bank in Joplin, Missouri to cash a check. Only the drive-in windows were open and the lines were long. As we waited our turn, the president of the bank, Harold E. Henson, walked up, recognized us, and slid into the car beside John, who was his pastor.

I facetiously asked, "Don't guess you know where I could get a check cashed, do you?"

"Maybe," he replied, "If I initial it."

I produced the check and he affixed his initials to it. We were in animated conversation when we arrived at the teller's window. The young lady at the window slid the drawer toward the car and I placed the check in it asking for cash. As she pulled the drawer to her she asked, "Sir, do you have an account in our bank?"

"No, I'm sorry I don't," I said.

The teller's drawer started back toward me as she said, "Sir, I'm sorry I can't cash your check."

"Not even with the bank president's initials on it?" I asked.

"Oh, yes!" she said as the drawer went back toward her.

I glanced to my right and there sat the president of the bank. I decided to make the most of the moment. "Would you not cash my check with the president of the bank sitting in my car?"

She bent down to peer through the window of my car and exclaimed, "Oh, Oh! Mr-r-r. Henson, Oh, yes sir! yes sir!" (The bank president had obviously not ridden with many customers to the drive-in windows.) I never got better service anywhere in my life.

The question "Do you have an account in our bank?" is always asked when you pray. Our response is always, "No, I don't, but I do come in the name of Jesus Christ." His name gives us the right to do business at the bank of heaven where all God's reserves of power are waiting to be distributed. Only the name of Jesus Christ is negotiable in prayer. Praying in the name of Jesus means praying according to all He is. No one knows all that Christ is as does the Holy Spirit. He directs in praying in the name of Jesus Christ, that we may claim all that He is for all that is needed. *"For the Son of God, Jesus Christ, who was preached among you by us . . . was not yea and nay, but in him was yea. For all the promises of God in him are yea, and in him Amen, unto the glory of God by us"* (2 Corinthians 1:19-20).

Not only do we have his very NAME in prayer, but we also have His very LIFE in prayer. The "president of the bank of heaven," Jesus Christ, indwells us through the Holy Spirit to direct the writing of checks. Our problem is not in writing checks that are too large because of insufficient funds; our problem is in writing checks that are too small because of insufficient faith. There are at least five accounts to draw from in prayer: adoration, thanksgiving, intercession, petition, and confession. The Holy Spirit directs not only to the account but to the amount.

> *Likewise the Spirit also helpeth our infirmities: for we know not what we should pray for as we ought: but the Spirit itself maketh intercession for us with groanings which cannot be uttered. And he that searcheth the hearts knoweth what is the mind of the Spirit, because he maketh intercession for the saints according to the will of God* (vs. 26, 27).

The universe yearns, the redeemed body yearns, and "likewise" the Holy Spirit yearns. In all probability, nothing yearns as does the Holy Spirit for that final restoration. As someone on special assignment to represent and produce holiness in the unholy culture of this world, how He indeed must yearn to complete the "drama of redemption." Knowing so well also the many Christian privileges not enjoyed, the many possessions never claimed, the many liberties never enjoyed, and all the other forfeitures of faithless Christians, how much He must yearn to move us into the heavenlies and the heavenlies into us. He must yearn with the strongest yearnings of all!

THE PROVISIONS OF EVERY CHRISTIAN

Romans 8:28–39

THE "ALLNESS" OF CHRIST

As the adventure of living "under new management" continues, we discover all the intricate preparations God has made on our behalf. *"Because Christ is all and in all"* (Colossians 3:11b), we see:

1. All Things Work Together For Good. *"And we know that all things work together for good to them that love God, to them who are the called according to his purpose"* (vs. 28). This verse has been glibly repeated so often in the face of adversity that some have concluded it's a "cop out" for a person who is a "dropout" from thinking. ALL THINGS DO WORK TOGETHER FOR GOOD because GOD'S IN CHARGE HERE. This doesn't mean that all things ARE good, nor does it mean that I turn cartwheels in my heart at everything that happens. It does mean that I have certified proof that God is at work, making everything that occurs in my life turn out for good. No matter how bad things may look, we can be confident in the final outcome as we remember that God hasn't finished working.

2. All Knowledge Conforms Us to Christ.

"For whom he did foreknow, he also did predestinate to be conformed to the image of his Son, that he might be the first born among many brethren" (vs. 29). God has never had a surprise. He knows all in His omniscience and thus foreknows all His awareness. "That surprises me!" has never once been heard in the councils of heaven. We are not "genetic accidents" but "regenerated persons" that God did predestine to be conformed to the spiritual specifications of Christ.

3. All Wisdom Planned our Lives. *"Moreover, whom he did predestinate, them he also called: and whom he called, them he also justified: and whom he justified, them he also glorified"* (vs. 30). Tragic indeed is the person who never discovers God's great plan for his life. More tragic still is the person who never sees the infinite Planner of life. God never has problems, only plans, because He is the Planner. He refuses to produce problems. He chooses to produce plans.

He predestinated (planned) for us to be who we are, where we are, that we might be made what He is, where He is. In His planning our lives, He calls us to Himself. We didn't come to Christ; He came to us. We didn't choose Christ; He chose us. We would have had no choice at all if He had not chosen to come to us and call. *"No man can come to me, except the Father which hath sent me draw him: and I will raise him up at the last day"* (John 6:44).

4. All Sufficiency Is Ours Because God Is For

Us. *"What shall we then say to these things? If God be for us, who can be against us?"* (Romans 8:31). We are indeed *"compassed about with so great a cloud of witnesses"* as we take the field to run *"the race that is set before us"* (Hebrews 12:1). Fr. R. G. Lee has observed, "If you get up in the morning, start your day and don't meet the devil, it's probably because you're going the same way he is." It makes no difference how early in the race you may meet the devil or any other enemy who's against you, you have GOD FOR YOU. We can move onward, *"looking unto Jesus the author and finisher of our faith"* (Hebrews 2:20). He is for us.

5. All Things Are Freely Given Us. *"He that spared not his own Son, but delivered him up for us all, how shall he not with him also freely give us all things?"* (vs. 32). One of the obvious reasons *"God loveth a cheerful* [hilarious] *giver"* (2 Corinthians 9:7b), is that He is a cheerful giver Himself. Christ was freely given. Christ freely gave. *"Not as the world gives give I unto you,"* He explained. Since all things are in Him, we have a generous flow of provisions being given to us at all times. Don't pray "Lord, bless me," but "Lord, make me blessable." Don't pray "Lord, give me," but "Lord, get me to where I can get what You're giving."

6. Our Record Is Clean. *"Who is he that condemneth?* [Shall] *Christ that died, yea rather, that is risen again, who is even at the right hand of*

God, who also maketh intercession for us" (vs. 34)? Where is the voice of condemnation coming from? Could Christ be seated now in power to act as our prosecutor? No, a thousand times no. He is not seated to condemn the saved. He will convict the saved, but not condemn. As a guarantor He is seated in intercession to keep our account clean. As we remain "confessed up to date," He guarantees that our record remains "all clean."

THE OCEANS OF GOD'S LOVE

The experience of resting in the love of God is like swimming in an ocean that doesn't even require your knowing how to swim. As faith buoys us up and carries us into the oceans of God's love, let us notice:

1. A Forfeit That Forsakes the Love of God. *"Who shall separate us from the love of Christ? Shall tribulation, or distress, or persecution, or famine, or nakedness, or peril, or sword?"* (vs. 35).

Before you answer the question WHAT SHALL SEPARATE US FROM THE LOVE OF GOD? with a resounding NOTHING, evaluate Jude 20 and 21: *"But ye, beloved, building up yourselves on your most holy faith, praying in the Holy [Spirit], keep yourselves in the love of God, looking for the mercy of our Lord Jesus Christ unto eternal life."* If you can KEEP YOURSELF IN THE LOVE OF GOD, it would logically follow that you can take yourself out of the love of God. Nothing can separate you from God's love outside of yourself. But YOU can! Whatever you may do, God will go on loving you unconditionally. Experientially you take yourself out of God. Reflection will bring you to realize that many people are living on the beaches of fear instead of floating in the ocean of love. When we take ourselves out of the ocean of God's love experientially, we always hit the beach of fear. The opposite of love is not hate, but fear. *"Perfect love casteth out fear, because fear hath [punishment]. He that feareth is not made perfect in love"* (1 John 4:18b). Hate is merely a form of fear. People hate as a defense mechanism because they fear. God does not treat the symptom but the disease; He casts out fear. If you're on the beach, God goes on loving you; get back into the ocean, yielding all you are to all He is.

One evening in a restaurant after a service, I was impressed to speak to the waitress about Christ. After a brief exchange of how the day had been a good one in Christ, I asked her if she knew Him.

"Yes, I met Christ years ago in Pennsylvania," was her very positive reply. "I went to church regularly for years, but you know I've not been in five years." She looked at me intently as if to see how I'd react when she said, "I'm so embarrassed that I don't go now."

"Do you know what I think that God must think of people who've not been to church in five years?" I asked.

"Oh, no! Don't tell me," she said and started to rush from the table.

"I think God loves them!" I asserted.

She stopped as if stabbed. "Well, why? Well, yes, I guess He does," she said ever so slowly as if it were too good to be true. For five years God had gone on loving her, but she had withdrawn from the ocean of realization.

2. A Faith that Conquers Through the Love of God. "*As it is written, For thy sake we are killed all the day long; we are accounted as sheep for the slaughter. Nay, in all these things we are more than conquerors through him that loved us*" (vs. 36, 37).

As sheep hearing His voice and following Him,

As sheep of His pasture feeding on the fullness of Him,

As sheep marked for slaughter, to the death we follow Him.

We go forth tagged as sheep for slaughter, yet we return crowned with the crowns of those made more than conquerors. We are "*Always bearing about in the body the dying of the Lord Jesus, that the life also of Jesus might be made manifest in our body. For we [who] live are always delivered unto death for Jesus' sake, that the life also of Jesus might be made manifest in our mortal flesh*" (2 Corinthians 4:10-11).

As the Lamb of God, He was gentle and meek.

As sheep, we go the second mile, turn the other cheek.

As the Lamb of God, He looked only on the Father to depend.
    As sheep complete in Him, we speak not ourselves to defend.
As the Lamb of God a conquering place upon a cross He took.
    As sheep, we're "more than conquerors"; 'tis written in the book.

Faith that rests only in Him is a faith that never rests, but spurs us on to be MORE THAN CONQUERORS as others *"Who through faith subdued kingdoms, wrought righteousness, obtained promises, stopped the mouths of lions, Quenched the violence of fire, escaped the edge of the sword, out of weakness were made strong, [became] valiant in fight, turned to flight the armies of the aliens"* (Hebrews 11:33-34).

3. A Fathomless Dimension in the Love of God.

As you relax your entire life into the person, power, and provisions of Jesus Christ, no experience can separate you from God's love. Paul was persuaded by that fact. His persuasion had not come from reading a good book, but out of experience. Experientially he knew that nothing can separate us from the love of God. Even man's most formidable foe, death, can't check the onrushing love of God.

It makes scriptural sense to me (and I am certain that I don't stand alone) that Paul knew the Love of God as a companion in the valley of the shadow of death, for he had been there. He was left for dead at Lystra (Acts 14:19). Could it be that he WAS dead? It can't be proved he was. Neither can it be PROVED he wasn't. What can be proved is that he once was in heaven. Approximately fourteen years after the experience at Lystra, he wrote,

> *I knew a man in Christ above fourteen years ago (whether in the body, I cannot tell; or whether out of the body, I cannot tell: God knoweth); such an one caught up to the third heaven* [the abode of God]. *And I knew such a man (whether in the body, or out of the body, I cannot tell: God knoweth); How that he was caught up into paradise, and heard unspeakable words, which it is not lawful for a man to utter. . . . And lest I should be exalted above measure through the abundance of the revelations, there was given to me a thorn in the flesh, the messenger of Satan to buffet me, lest I should be exalted above measure* (2 Corinthians 12:2-4, 7).

Through what avenue—in the body or out of the body—Paul got to heaven, I don't know, but he did get there. Just as Lazarus was called back into his body by Jesus, Paul was sent back into his body or with his body. He was sent back to minister until the final call.

See all the other dimensions that God's love covers like a swelling tide:

DEATH   LIFE

ANGELS   PRINCIPALITIES

POWERS

HEIGHT   DEPTH

ANY CREATION

"The love of God is greater far
    Than tongue or pen can ever tell;
It goes beyond the highest star,
    And reaches to the lowest hell:
The guilty pair, bowed down with care,
    God gave His Son to win;
His erring child He reconciled,
    And pardoned from his sin.

Could I with ink the ocean fill,
    Were the whole sky of parchment made,
Were every blade of grass a quill
    And every man a scribe by trade;
To write the love of God above
    Would drain the ocean dry;
Nor could the scroll contain the whole
    Though spread from sky to sky.

Oh, love of God, how rich and pure!
    How measureless and strong!

It shall forevermore endure—
  The saints' and angels' song."

F. M. Lehman
Copyright 1917. Renewed 1945
by Nazarene Publishing
House. Used by permission.

THE PURSUIT OF EVERY CHRISTIAN

Romans 9:1–3

As the life of Christ becomes the life of a Christian, the pursuit of Christ becomes the pursuit of a Christian. After Jesus had called Zacchaeus down out of the tree and made the littlest man around the happiest man in town by saving him, Christ then announced the mission of His life: *"For the son of man is come to seek and to save that which was lost"* (Luke 19:10). Though multiple were the ministries He performed, nothing ever deterred Him from that ultimate aim.

Why come to a Christ-controlled stance in life today? Why should Jesus Christ be reproduced in us by the Holy Spirit who produced His earthly life 1900 years ago? Is it to have the good, warm feeling reported by many? Is it to get rid of our hang-ups and be the integrated personality that psychologists advocate? Is it to obtain a testimony we can give at the next testimony time?

While some or all of these results may occur in us, we come under Christ's control that He may resume His pursuits in us today. His mission has not altered; He is still seeking and saving those who are lost.

THREE EXAMPLES OF DIVINE COMPASSION IN HUMAN LIVES

Three men in Scripture were taken by the Lord to such a place of compassion for the people about them that they offered to be cast into hell themselves if only the people could be spared.

1. Moses: When he returned from being in the presence of God on Sinai he saw the debauchery of a people who had just left four hundred years of slavery in Egypt and were now the slaves of sin and vice. Before the Lord, knowing full well the consequences of his request, he asked for his name to be stricken from the Lamb's book of life if the people could be saved (Exodus 32:32).

2. Christ: He prayed in the garden that the cup of sin that He in His sinlessness would have to drink might pass from Him. "*Nevertheless, not my will but thine be done*," He affirmed. He did not want the cup, but ever so much He did want the will of the Father. This was no ordinary prayer meeting. Knowing full well that to drink the cup was to drink in the nature of all man's sins and thus pay the price of separation from God, He affirmed, "THY WILL BE DONE." The Christ of God, who through all His eternal existence had strolled in the glory of heaven, was willing now to be made sin and of necessity to slump to the agony of hell.

3. Paul: He was so moved by the compassion of the same indwelling Christ that he also was willing to be accursed if his fellow Jews could be

saved. *"I say the truth in Christ, I lie not, my con-science also bearing me witness in the Holy [Spirit], That I have great heaviness and contin-ual sorrow in my heart. For I could wish that I myself were accursed from Christ for my breth-ren, my kinsmen according to the flesh"* (Romans 9:1-3).

As I write beyond chapter eight of Romans, I must write beyond where I have gone in my own laboratory experiences. I know little experientially of the burden that Paul describes here, though smaller samplings have lain like weights on my heart at times. We should never assume that Paul's experience here is to be ours identically any more than being blinded three days is necessary in order to be saved, or being in heaven and then returning to earth must be our experience if we are to go where Christ wants to take us. Yet Christ's own compassion will in greater or lesser degrees be part of our life style in bringing others to know peace with God. Since I'm beyond my own experience I'll invite you to read Paul's lab report with me:

A WITNESSING CONSCIENCE. *"I say the truth in Christ, I lie not, my conscience also bearing me witness in the Holy [Spirit]"* (Romans 9:1). It seems that Paul can hardly believe his own attitude toward the lost, and he must affirm a clear con-science before the Holy Spirit that what he is relat-ing is spiritually valid if the Christians in Rome are to believe his report. It's like someone saying, "No lie now, this is what happened." When that cliché is used it implies that the listener will find it hard to believe what will be said. What Paul is about to relate is so far removed from most experiences that the readers in Rome had to be prepared.

A WEIGHTY COMPASSION. *"I have great heaviness and continual sorrow in my heart"* (vs. 2). Upon Paul rested the same spiritual heaviness that Jesus felt when, weeping, He looked over a city dwelling in spiritual death needing spiritual life. That same Holy Spirit heaviness has sent thousands out of themselves, out of their public image, out of their securities, and even out of their own countries to tell others that He is the Way, the Truth, and the Life.

I recently spent part of a weekend with two such witnesses who have moved out of themselves, their public image, and their securities on to another nation to share Christ's life. As the compassion of Christ constrained Dr. and Mrs. Ted Garrison of Camdenton, Missouri, they accepted God's promotion from an outstanding medical practice to find real satisfaction in sharing Christ with others in Seoul, Korea. In two years there, they, along with the medical team they directed, saw over four thousand people come to Christ and over thirty thousand of Korea's needy people receive better physical health, as well as spiritual life. They went, not without struggle, not without tears, but not without *"the joy that was set before Him"* either, which is the joy of seeing Christ enter others to be their life. After two years of the

JOY SET BEFORE THEM, Ted and Loretta Garrison testify: *"And being fully [assured] that what he had promised, he was able also to perform"* (Romans 4:21).

A WISTFUL CONDEMNATION. *"For I could wish that myself were accursed from Christ for my brethren, my kinsmen according to the flesh"* (vs. 3). Paul was willing to be consigned to perdition, if by so doing he could prevent others from following. Yet what he proposed could not be, for he himself had already been made alive forever in Christ. Even if he could go to hell, he could not stop others; only their receiving safety in Christ personally could stop them from going to eternal destruction.

Such an agony of heart is illustrated in a recently returned P.O.W. from Viet Nam. As one of the courageous men of our nation who languished seven long years in prison, Howard Reutledge tells how he finally was freed and landed in the Philippines. After the merciless treatment of the prison at Hanoi, he says the hardest blow of all came during his first phone call with his wife. Anticipating seeing all his family, he was already envisioning Johnny as a strong athlete. But Phyllis said, "Howard, I must tell you something. Johnny went swimming the first year you were in prison, dived off the coast, and struck a rock just under the water. He's a quadriplegic and will never walk." He says in his book *In the Presence of Mine Enemies*, he would have returned to Hanoi to die in that prison if only Johnny could have left his prison of paralysis.

Only one man could do what that inner compulsion of the Spirit had laid upon His heart. Christ alone could plunge to the lowest levels of hell—separation from God (Matthew 27:46) and return in triumph to be elevated to the highest heights of heaven (Ephesians 1:20-21). Dr. Henry Morris gives a vivid picture of the death of Christ on our behalf:

A most intriguing illustration of this is found in the twenty-second Psalm, that marvelous prophetic description of the suffering and death of Christ on the cross, written a thousand years before its fulfillment. In the midst of His sufferings, the Lord Jesus cries in His heart: *But I am a worm, and no man; a reproach of men, and despised of the people* (Psalm 22:6).

In the parallel prophecy of Isaiah, it was said *that His visage was so marred* (in fact, literally, 'Corruption' personified) *more than any man, and his form more than the sons of men* (Isaiah 53:3). But in what sense could He have been said actually to be a worm?

In ancient Israel, as in the modern world, there were many types of worms, of course, and several different kinds are mentioned in the Bible. But the worm referred to in Psalm 22:6 was a special worm known as the "scarlet worm." It was from this worm that a valuable secretion was obtained with which to make scarlet dyes. As a matter of fact, the same word is sometimes translated by "scarlet" or "crimson."

When the female of the scarlet worm species was ready to give birth to her young, she would attach her body to the trunk of a tree, fixing herself so firmly and permanently that she could never leave again. The eggs deposited beneath her body were thus protected until the larvae were hatched and able to leave and enter their own life cycle. As the mother died, the crimson fluid stained her body and the surrounding wood. From the dead bodies of such female scarlet worms, the commercial scarlet dyes of antiquity were extracted.

And what a picture this gives of Christ, dying on the Tree, shedding His precious blood, that He might *bring many sons unto glory* (Hebrews 2:10).

THE TESTIMONY OF A MODERN SOUL WINNER

The man God used years ago to share with Billy Graham the principles of the Spirit-filled life was Dr. Stephen F. Olford. Billy Graham has gone on to be without peer in introducing men to Christ. Dr. Olford gives his testimony in the introduction to a classical book on soul winning that I strongly recommend, *The Secret of Soul Winning*:

Does the subject of personal soul-winning frighten you? If it does, you have my sympathy! I say that because I know from experience what you are passing through. There was a time in my life when even the thought of talking to people, publicly or privately, paralyzed me with fear. I was not only painfully shy by nature but hopelessly indisposed to meeting new faces. Many a social occasion in our home was spoiled because of my unannounced disappearance!

The fact that I was a committed Christian did not seem to make much difference. In one sense, it made me worse. As a saved person, I knew it was my duty to witness for my Lord and, when possible, to seek to win others to Him. But such a sense of duty only brought me into inner bondage. I have known what it is to screw up my courage and walk the entire length of a train giving out gospel booklets to anyone who was courteous enough (and, I often thought, pitying enough) to take a copy. But was I ever glad when such a task was completed!

It was not as if I had not read books on soul-winning. As it happened, I had a wide selection of works on the subject, and often I perused them in the hope of finding the secret to successful soul-winning.

Then God graciously stepped in. He had permitted me to struggle on long enough to convince me that I could do nothing about it. I was shy; I was bound; and I was defeated. In a word, I was a failure.

I began to see—slowly but clearly—that SOUL-WINNING IS GOD'S WORK. From the start to the finish He must plan and carry it through. My business is to be in line with His will. Winning men and women to the Lord Jesus Christ is not a matter of trial and error but of being led by the Holy Spirit. *"For as many as are led by the Spirit of God, they are the Sons of God"* (Romans 8:14).

Shortly after this, I attended a convention. A much-used servant of God was expounding John 7:37-39. Something he said arrested me. As nearly as I can remember, these were his words: "There is only one successful Soul-Winner, and that is the Lord Jesus Christ. To try to copy him is to fail miserably; for His thoughts are not our thoughts; neither are His ways our ways. If we would succeed in this great task of winning the lost to God, then Jesus must work in us and through us, by the power of His Spirit. Listen to His own words:

'*He that believeth on me, as the scripture hath said, out of his innermost being shall flow rivers of living water. (This spake he of the spirit, which they that believe on him should receive: for the Holy Ghost was not yet given; because that Jesus was not yet glorified.)*' Only as we believe IN Him and allow Him to flow through us by His Spirit will men and women whom He is drawing to Himself respond. To the Spirit-led child of God, this will mean liberty, joy, and blessing in the work of personal evangelism."

That evening I went home determined to cease trying and to start trusting. From that moment soul-winning for me has been different. Not only have I been delivered from shyness and self-consciousness, but I have been introduced to a level of soul-winning which is divinely directed and unspeakably joyous.

I have failed since—many times; but always I have known the reason—and the way of restoration! The Lord Jesus is the only successful Soul-Winner, and it is only when He is in complete control of my life that I can hope to share in the fruits of His labors.

Such surrender to His sovereignty does not necessarily imply or guarantee on-the-spot decisions for Christ every time a person is approached on the subject! We certainly are called upon to preach the gospel to every creature; but the Lord adds to His Church only *such as should be* (or, are being) *saved* (Acts 2:47). This is a deep mystery, but it is a fact of Scripture and of personal experience.

What happens is that, as we witness in the power of the Spirit to all and sundry, some soul is especially laid upon our hearts. Like Philip of old, we are bidden (inwardly) to "go near and join" ourselves to this person. Sometimes this results at once in a conversion. Then there are other occasions when that honor is reserved for someone else. In either instance, however, the issue from the divine standpoint is certain and successful. What matters supremely is that we are LED BY THE SPIRIT OF GOD.

THE BLESSING OF BALANCE

The contemporary scene of soul winning, or lack of it, reminds me of an experience in Delhi, India, several years ago. After speaking on Sunday morning in one of the few large churches in north India, I was invited by the pastor to attend a committee meeting. Though I accepted, the language barrier locked me out of the discussion. It was not unlike some I'd witnessed in the states. One man was mad, one man was glad, and the rest seemed to be trying to decide whether to be mad or glad. After thirty minutes of heated argument the pastor said with embarrassment, "They're debating whether to serve dark or light tea at the banquet."

In a nation of wall-to-wall people with only 2% professing to know Christ in their capital city of 4 to 5 million, and half of them never having heard who Jesus Christ is, they debated over whether to serve dark or light tea at a banquet!

In America today the scene is much the same. Some advocate "going deeper" (dark tea) and some advocate "going steeper" (light tea); Jesus advocates "going to all." Some have gone so deep, they have forgotten that most people haven't found the front door yet, let alone the banquet rooms. Just stand outside with bubble gum, bicycles, and even new cars as "door prizes" and "compel them to come in." They're finding the bubble gum gets stale, the bicycles break down, and even the car wears out. What's the answer? A balanced life, of course, Christ alone, yet Christ always, brings balance! It's not an "either-or" but both!

A few years ago a railway executive flew over the tracks in Canada to inspect the line from the air. In the most remote part of the wild terrain, the motor of the plane failed. He got the plane down on the only cleared place, the track, without injury to himself. Miles separated him from the nearest depot, but knowing that if he were to survive he must get there, he set out.

Hour after hour he walked the track. Nearing exhaustion, hands and face freezing, he began thinking about the big pot-bellied stove glowing red hot in the depot. He quickened his pace and an hour later reached the depot and stepped inside. The red hot stove was grey cold, so a "red hot" executive shouted at the depot operator, "Why haven't you built a fire in the stove?"

"Sir, I've been so busy sending messages on this teletype, I just haven't had time!"

"Then send another," he snapped. "Wire the main office two words, 'You're fired!' " Thirty minutes later he asked, "Did you send the message?"

"No, sir, I've been too busy building a fire!"

If we're balanced, we'll build fires of spiritual warmth and send out messages of spiritual life all at the same time.

Get Balanced
Get Blessed   **Get Blessed**
                                              Get Balanced

| THE WAY | THE TRUTH | THE LIFE |

```
            /\
           /C \
          / H  \
         /  R   \
        /   I    \
       /    S     \
      /     T      \
     /_____\
```

POSTSCRIPT

My role as tour guide through three chapters and three verses of Romans must end here. At least 150 times before, I've led tours among these truths, as stated in the introduction, but this trip has been the most meaningful of all to me. Pausing at places where I'd never lingered before, I've viewed truths never seen before. Another 150 tours later I'm sure I'll still be seeing MUCH MORE and even MUCH, MUCH MORE. Family and friends who have heard me give these studies repeatedly have never heard portions of the book at all, so new have these latest "finds" been. In fact, some may wonder if a "ghost writer" assisted me. So distinctive has been the enjoyment and enrichment accompanying the writings that I trust the Holy "Ghost Writer" has been in both the desire and direction of writing.

I need not tell you there's still MUCH MORE in the redemptive romance of Romans . . . so don't miss it! As a final farewell, I want to wish this blessing on you as you go in the WAY, the TRUTH, and the LIFE. . . .

Only be thou strong and very courageous, that thou mayest observe to do according to all the law . . . turn not from it to the right hand or to the left, that thou mayest prosper (wherever) thou goest. This book of the law shall not depart out of thy mouth; but thou shalt meditate therein day and night . . . then thou shall make thy way prosperous, and then thou shalt have good success (Joshua 1:7-8).

KEEP GOING——THERE IS
MUCH, MUCH, MUCH MORE AHEAD
If You're
JUST DYING TO LIVE